"Perhaps one of the main reasons I love the country that raised me is the rich diversity of people attracted to its vast and challenging open spaces and the characters spawned from the mix.

All too often we cross paths with these characters in the most unlikely of places. Their intriguing pasts excite us with stories stretching, most often, from across the oceans to different worlds. This story provides an exotic beginning in a small far away island that would sit comfortably in most fairy tales.

Elizabeth Kempster, being a close friend of my mother, is the embodiment of an enduring character — the pioneering outback mother, pilot and entrepreneur. A victorious battler of this challenging land.

"Ian had told me that he always wanted to go to Australia, so a few days after we were married we flew to Sydney — I did not think it would be a lifelong change."

This book brings to life an engaging tale of a family taking on the challenges of a growing Australia. Elizabeth's life has embedded itself as part of the rich mosaic of colourful characters giving this country its soul.

A thoroughly engaging read."

— Rob Katter, MP, State Member For Traeger

"In every generation there are people who live extraordinary lives — and Elizabeth Kempster is certainly one of those whose life has not been ordinary. Born in the immediate aftermath on World War II on the island of Jersey, her childhood was idyllic, and she could have chosen to live on that pleasant and beautiful island, which still means so much to her. But after marrying her childhood sweetheart in 1968, they moved to Australia and the adventure begun. A honeymoon spent in a baby-blue Landrover crossing Australia, they eventually ended up in rural Western Australia, raising a family of four boys.

However, it was not to a fairy-tale — with her husband turning to grog, the marriage collapsed and Elizabeth had to make her own way in life. Tragedies, trials and hardships followed: her son Grant was badly burnt in an accident at the age of eight; her marriage could not be saved; and bankruptcy. For Elizabeth, as for many of us, life is not a simple series of upward advances. But fortunately life is more than just the sum of successes and failures. The life well-lived is not one of success, but one of love.

In her latter years, Elizabeth has found her way to Charters Towers — a long way from her home in Jersey, which still clearly means so much to Elizabeth. But home is also to be found in Charters Towers, for home is not just a physical location. With her sons grown up, with grandchildren, and with friends: home is where love is and in that love is found joy. I commend this book to you: a story of faith and of love. If you are looking for a book about success and advancement in life, this is not it. This is not some sort of triumphant recounting of an easy life. But it is the story of a woman who has true achievements and blessings: a strong sense of place, of family and of love. Enjoy the *Memoirs of Jersey Girl*."

— The Right Revd Dr Keith Joseph
Bishop of North Queensland

"*Memoirs of a Jersey Girl* provides an amazing account of a life lived to the full, from a childhood in Nazi-occupied Jersey to raising a family with the barest of home essentials deep in the Australian outback, through bankruptcy, tragedy and joy; adventures as a competition pilot and more. It is both touching and inspiring, and themes of family, determination, love and commitment shine through every chapter.

A recommended read for anyone who is intrigued by the human story."
— Squadron Leader Justin Paines, RAF Rtd., Test Pilot

"In *Memoirs of a Jersey Girl*, Elizabeth Kempster has produced a very inspiring family history passing on her strong values of love, integrity and honesty without specifically dwelling on those values but, rather, by living them throughout the ups and downs of her often very challenging life. Her resilience in the face of adversity is supported by a subtle sense of humour and by travel in a world beyond her own doorstep which excites her sense of adventure. I'm sure this book will be highly valued by family in years to come. Thank you Elizabeth for sharing your journey with other readers. Your story has been of particular interest to me as I have historical family ties to Jersey and have been born and bred in an Australian farming family."
— Jenni Greenham, author of *A Cloudy Path*

Memoirs of a Jersey Girl

Elizabeth Kempster

Published in Australia by Sid Harta Books & Print Pty Ltd,
ABN: 34632585293
23 Stirling Crescent, Glen Waverley, Victoria 3150 Australia
Telephone: +61 3 9560 9920, Facsimile: +61 3 9545 1742
E-mail: author@sidharta.com.au

First published in Australia 2021
This edition published 2021
Copyright © Elizabeth Kempster 2021
Cover design, typesetting: WorkingType (www.workingtype.com.au)

The right of Elizabeth Kempster to be identified as the Author of the Work has been asserted in accordance with the Copyright, Designs and Patents Act 1988.

All rights reserved. No part of this publication may be reproduced, stored in a retrieval system, or transmitted, in any form or by any means without the prior written permission of the publisher, nor be otherwise circulated in any form of binding or cover other than that in which it is published and without a similar condition being imposed on the subsequent purchaser.

Kempster, Elizabeth
Memoirs of a Jersey Girl
ISBN: 978-1-925707-50-2
pp290

Elizabeth Kempster hails from the island of Jersey, in the Channel Islands. She comes from generations of farmers and the land is in her blood. After her marriage Elizabeth emigrated to Australia, travelled up the east coast and worked at Fort Constantine, Cloncurry. She and her husband made their way over to Western Australia where they settled on a farm in Boyup Brook, south of Perth. Due to unforeseen circumstances they moved up to the north-east of the state and lived on sheep and cattle stations in Western Australia for many years, where they raised a family of four boys. Elizabeth re-settled with her sons in Queensland in the 1980s and now calls Charters Towers her home. She was inspired to write this memoir to preserve her family history for succeeding generations, in particular her grandchildren, as family connections tend to fade with time. She hopes they will take pride in their heritage, as she does in hers.

For my family, in particular my grandchildren, Harrison, Thomas, Claire, Lillian, Patrick and Joni.

To Chloe, who taught me how to tackle the daunting task of responding to the editor's suggestions on my computer.

To Kylie, who showed me how to use "control c" and "control v".

To Bronwin Dargaville, my editor, who was meticulous in putting my ramblings in the correct order and polishing my writing.

To Luke Harris, my design editor, for putting together a great book cover and layout.

To Kerry B. Collison, who took on my story and published it.

To Zak, Warren, Grant and Adrian who gave me the resolve to keep going.

Finally, to my grandchildren for whom the story was told.

Foreword

This is the captivating story of a young woman, originally from the tiny island of Jersey in the English Channel, and her "Adonis", as they emigrate to Australia to follow their romantic dream. But disappointment awaits them and their farming plans are dashed.

Facing life's many obstacles, first as a couple then as a single mother of four sons, Elizabeth threw herself into every challenge — whether it was helping to run pastoral stations many times larger than her native island, winning competitions in horse riding, becoming a proficient pilot or, later, achieving success in business ventures in her own right.

The delights and misfortunes of Elizabeth's remarkable life are vividly described as the chapters of this Australian odyssey unfold, all the while her indomitable spirit carrying her through. Yet, most important to Elizabeth, and underpinning her whole existence, has been her dedication to family and their wellbeing.

This fascinating and moving memoir of a Jersey girl making a success of life in her adopted Australia is sure to stimulate and entertain; I heartily recommend it as a most enjoyable read.

Derrick Frigot, MBE, ARAgS
Patron, World Jersey Cattle Bureau

Contents

Introduction		1
Chapter 1	1940–1945	6
Chapter 2	1960–1968	36
Chapter 3	1968–1970	63
Chapter 4	1971–1973	77
Chapter 5	1974–1975 Station Life	81
Chapter 6	1976–1980	88
Chapter 7	1981 continued	111
Chapter 8	1983	116
Chapter 9	Late 1985	126
Chapter 10	1986–1994	129
Chapter 11	1986–1994 continued	145
Chapter 12	1994–2001	158
Chapter 13	2001–2008	164
Chapter 14	2009	198
Chapter 15	2012	204
Chapter 16	2012 continued	214
Chapter 17	2013	218
Chapter 18	2013 continued	228
Chapter 19	2014	238
Chapter 20	2014–2015	252
Chapter 21	2016–2020	261
Conclusion		271

Introduction

A short history of the island of Jersey

Around 6000 BC Jersey became an island after splitting from the Normandy peninsula. Then around 4000 BC, during the Neolithic period, communities settled and made their home in Jersey. Many of the island's standing gravestones and burial chambers date from these times.

During the ninth century AD Vikings plundered the island, gave 'Jersey' its name, settled on the Cotentin Coast and named the Duchy of Normandy, in France.

In 555 AD the hermit St Helier, who gave Jersey's capital its name and who lived on a small rocky islet near Elizabeth Castle, was murdered by raiders.

My mother's maiden name, de Gruchy (spelt de

Grouchy in France) originates from Grouchy on the border of Cotentin and Bessin. This area was granted 'en fief' to the Viking settlers on the creation of the state of Normandy. From near Carantan, the Knights Nicholas and Guillaume de Grouchy rode off on the First Crusade, being present at the fall of Jerusalem.

In about 1204 the de Grouchys scattered when the French kings took over Normandy. The de Grouchy sons Jean and Guillaume settled in Jersey and the family was established there by the end of the thirteenth century.

The Billots were first recorded in Jersey in 1331. They came from Normandy—a little place called Pont Billot, near Lisieux.

Each region developed its own language, or patois, and Jerriais is the Jersey language. The olde laws are written in this Jersey French, which my parents spoke at home. They used to speak very quickly when there was something they didn't want me to understand and I distinctly remember my father uttering these words: 'tchi bougre p'tit mousse', when I'd done something naughty. This translates as 'little beggar of a child'. By the early 1900s English was the common language spoken in St Helier and gradually overtook Jersey French in the country.

Thomas Philippe's son Alfred Samuel farmed at Carmel, Trinity, in which parish he was Inspecteur des Chemins for Rozel and Procureur du Bien Public, another son Philip Durell farmed at Highfield, Trinity, whilst other descendants have lived in St. John, St. Mary, St. Ouen and at Cowley, St. Saviour ! It may be noted that his son Francis William married four times! Francis William's eldest son, Francis Philip, settled in Canada, where he has descendants. Another son, Clifford Clarence, represented his parish as a Deputy in the States of Jersey. Jean Thomas [GN3] returned to Australia, married a Miss Casey and was the father of William (a commercial traveller who married Susanna de Villiers when in South Africa in 1905), Thomas, Claud, Harold, Blanche and Florence. Thomas was a chemist and father of Dr Carl de Gruchy, the eminent haematologist and author.

Alfred Samuel de Gruchy [Tree GN] of Carmel Farm, Rozel (T) and Georgina Binet his wife - courtesy of Mrs E. Billot.

Francis William de Gruchy [Tree GN] on his International Tractor 1930s - courtesy of Mrs B.S. Le Cornu

Extract from The de Gruchys of Jersey *by Walter J Le Quesne and Guy Dixon. Reproduced with permission. Top photo: Elizabeth's grandparents, Grandpa and Grandma de Gruchy*

Four generations of St Martin Billots in 1932: standing (left to right)—my father Thomas, Grandpa Charles; seated—great grandmother Lydie (nee Tourgis) with my sister Anne on her lap. Both Charles and Thomas were Constables of the parish. See 'Descendants of Elie Billot' at https://www.theislandwiki.org/index.php/Descendants_of_Elie_Billot_-_2

Jersey is the largest of the Channel Islands situated in the bay of St Malo and is twenty kilometres from the French coast. It is eight kilometres long, fourteen and a half kilometres wide and has a population of around 98 000 people. It is divided into twelve parishes and is self-governed by the States Assembly which comprises forty-nine elected members. The Billot family hails from the Parish of St Martin. Today, Jersey is a British Crown Dependency and the Lieutenant-Governor is the personal representative of the Queen.

Chapter 1
1940-1945

I was born after the Second World War into a Jersey farming family. I begin my memoir on the island of Jersey, my childhood home, which stills holds a special place in my heart and to which I remain connected.

The Channel Islands had been occupied by the German Armed Forces for most of the war. Though I hadn't yet been born, I know of the hardships they endured during the war under the German occupation, and tales of this time form a significant part of our family's history. My mother and father took risks such as keeping a radio hidden and listening to the BBC, which was verboten. My mother made mittens out of rabbit skins to keep warm. The rabbits, kept in hutches, fed the family until they were stolen. My Aunty Lily and Uncle Charlie kept a pig hidden in the cellar.

Tank traps at low tide to stop allied shipping from entering at Rozel Bay, during the occupation of Jersey, 1945

My father endured the pain and discomfort of double pneumonia culminating in a collapsed lung. My mother gave him all the loving care necessary to keep him alive. This, together with trying to keep the farm running and looking after three little girls, was a daunting task.

Liberation Day on 9 May 1945 was greeted with much relief and joy. The young girls in my family danced around the flagpole with laughter and glee in the front garden of our home at La Ville Bree. Any feelings of happiness, previously curtailed by the invaders' presence, were now free to express themselves.

Girls dancing around flagpole celebrating Liberation Day 9 May 1945 at La Ville Bree, St Martin

My father, Thomas George Billot, was sent to London and operated on by Sir Clement Price Thomas of Harley Street. This was the first successful operation of its kind, which left my father with only one lung and a huge scar across his chest. Consequently, Dad regularly sent a box of Jersey new potatoes each spring harvest to Sir Clement in gratitude. Sir Clement had also operated on King George VI, so Dad had the best of care.

Life returned to normal—or as normal as

possible with an incapacitated head of the family who was limited in the physical work he could do. His foreman, Jack Rouault, was a small but capable worker. He was known within the family as Bow Wow (I think he used to bark orders) and his wife, Missus, helped Mum in the house.

1945-1953

Dad was renowned for his cattle breeding expertise. He exported many offspring of Visiting Design, who was a Jersey champion for a number of years. Countries such as the United States, South Africa and New Zealand would today have descendants from this wonderful cow.

I was born on 11 July 1948, Elizabeth Eunice Billot, to Eunice Beatrice Billot (nee de Gruchy). At age forty my parents were aghast to find out another child would be joining the family. There would be a gap of sixteen years between Anne Elizabeth, fifteen years between Ruth Mary and fourteen years between Mary Gertrude and myself. I was a Caesarean baby. Childbirth did not come easily to my mother. Dad nearly lost Mum during childbirth with their firstborn, a son, who could not be saved. It still grieves me that, in those days, my brother could not be buried in the family grave. An unknown, unmarked plot in St Martin's cemetery was his first and final resting place.

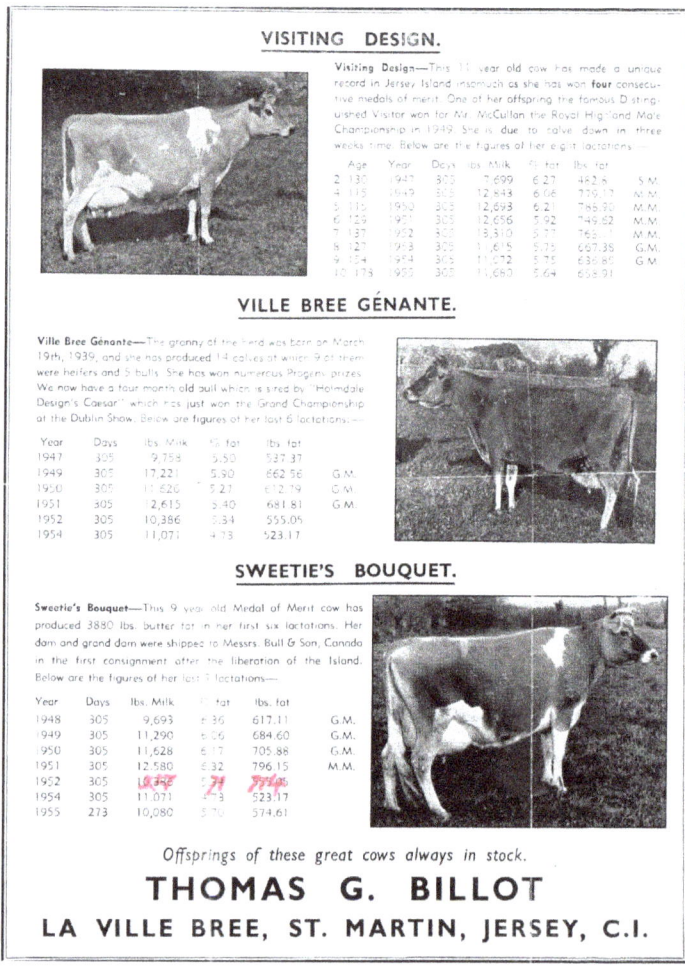

Dad's flyer promoting his Jersey cows' pedigree and offspring

Milking time—no milking machines

Elizabeth milking by hand

Painting of my sister Anne bringing the cows in for milking at La Ville Bree

La Ville Bree (Elizabeth on front wall)

Elizabeth's Christening

I had a carefree upbringing, which I believe was partially the result of a release from the suppression which my parents had endured during the war. At least, my three sisters believed I lacked discipline!

My first recollection was sitting on the edge of Grandmother de Gruchy's tall bed. She had been ill. Bearing ten children had taken its toll. I slipped off and fell into the electric bar heater, burning my right foot. I still have the scar and that was the last time I saw her.

My second recollection was of Dad taking me to Mrs Ahier's kindergarten, 'Springside,' on the tractor. At three years of age I was not prepared to be separated from my parents. I remember shaking the enormous double wrought iron gates and screaming my head off at Dad not to leave me. I'm sure that's why Mum didn't take me as she knew there'd be a scene. I never forgave poor Dad!

I began riding at an early age. Dad used to put me on horses before I could walk and so my love of horses began and consumed my life until I became a teenager.

Elizabeth's first ride

Elizabeth at eighteen months

I began riding Prince, a sixteen hand ex German warhorse, who was terrified of most things. The Germans had taken Dad's good horse, Dolly, and given him this nervous wreck in exchange. However, with time and kindness I was able to ride him unaided and even taught him to jump. I used to scarify the new potatoes with him, but he would tread on a number of plants due to his large hooves and wide gait.

Prince (1947) *Prince (1960)*

Life was full of fun and adventure. In 1953, at five years of age, I was placed in the Jersey Young Farmers float at the Battle of Flowers, which is a local Jersey carnival held annually in August to celebrate the coronation of King Edward VII and Queen Alexandra. I was sitting in an enormous basket adorned with beautiful fresh flowers. Each parish and many social clubs spent hours upon hours designing and fabricating enormous floats of all themes, from *The Lion King* to *Rocket to the Moon*. Work began twelve months in advance, and a few days prior to the event, fresh flowers grown especially for the occasion were inserted into the wire which covered the frames of the vehicles. These spectacular mobile floats paraded in the Jersey Battle of Flowers, which was a huge boost to tourism. Sunny Jersey was quite the rage with British tourists for many years.

Elizabeth in basket of flowers in an exhibit at the Battle of Flowers (1952)

Also at five years of age, Mum took me to Madame Le Riche's Dancing School. Mum used to enjoy taking me to the eisteddfods in Jersey and Guernsey. I used to love going to Guernsey because I would get to sleep in Mum's double bed in the guest house there. I was good at national/character dancing and won a few trophies. I was also selected to dance the lead role at the annual pantomimes held at the Jersey Theatre. I remember a member of the audience taking me to his toy shop in St Helier and telling me I could choose anything I wanted. I was not 'into' toys but chose a huge doll that was standing in the corner. I took her home and she stood in my bedroom corner for as long as I can remember. I preferred to dress up the farm kittens, putting them in my doll's pram and smacking them when they jumped out. Poor little things!

I really enjoyed dancing and went through the grades until I was eleven years of age, when our family doctor advised to choose either dancing or riding because of the stomach pains I was experiencing. Of course, horses won the day.

I was very close to my nephews Robbie and Phil Perchard, who were just a few years younger than me. I remember acting as school teacher in the anemone room, a little storeroom where we kept baby piglets under an infrared lamp and bunched anemones for sale in winter.

We happened to have an old wooden desk complete with ink wells. Robbie told me I was a good teacher. This experience was to stand me in good stead for one of the roles I played later in life. Robbie and Phil were the two gorgeous pageboys and

I was the bridesmaid at my sister Mary's wedding to Robert Lacey. We re-enacted the scene at Mary and Bob's ruby wedding anniversary celebration, held at The Golden Lion in Napsbury, Hertfordshire, England, forty years later.

Mum, Elizabeth and kitten

Guernsey eisteddfod (1955). Elizabeth (right) tied for first place

*Mother Goose pantomime held in Jersey Opera House,
Christmas 1959*

Top: Elizabeth second from left

Bottom: Elizabeth third from left (back row)

Robbie, Elizabeth, Philip 1996 (left to right)

Philip, Elizabeth, Robbie (1956)

1953-1959

My carefree lifestyle ended when I was sent to Jersey High School on Stopford Road. The discipline and ritual of school life did not appeal to me. One day my cousin, Rosemary Ahier, and myself decided to change the school clocks so we could get out early. Well, what an eruption ensued! I had never seen my mother so furious. Our head mistress, Mrs Harman, boxed my ears! Rosemary's parents just laughed. We were lucky not to get expelled. I don't think Mum came to terms with how naughty I'd been.

I was given the opportunity of riding Magpie, a little piebald pony that the Pearce family, who were friends of my parents, had grown out of. I used to ride my bike to St Ouen's, five miles away, in order to ride her. My school friend Pat Renouard and I won first prize in musical pairs at Springfield Gymkhana in August 1959.

Springfield Gymkhana 1959. Elizabeth with rosette in mouth and Patricia behind

When my parents saw that riding wasn't a passing fad, they bought me a Welsh mountain pony of my own from one of the riding schools. Kit, although a pretty dapple grey, was a nasty piece of work and would kick or bite to get out of being ridden. Needless to say, we didn't have her for long.

I was lent a pony, Cindy, from Steve Perchard who emigrated to New Zealand, together with his family. Cindy was a beautiful 12.2 hand roan. She had been neglected. Her hooves were curled like Egyptian slippers. I used to love taking her to the blacksmith and watch him make shoes for her by heating the steel in the forge and hammering them into shape on the anvil. He would then mould them onto her feet, and the burning of red-hot steel against hoof is a memory I can still see and smell. Cindy had a mouth like iron, so at the shows I'd point her at the jumps and she'd just fly over them. She was fabulous and we always vied for first place with Rosemary (my cousin from school) riding Cromus, a little skewbald pony who was Cindy's equal.

Elizabeth jumping over potato boxes on Kit

I taught my nephew, Philip, to ride. By this stage, with Philip having grown, Cindy was just his size and was gifted to him by his Uncle Steve. This left me horseless. I persuaded Mum to take me to The New Forest in order to purchase an unbroken pony at the local sales. The idea was for me to break in the pony and sell it, therefore making it a good investment for my parents!

When we were there I spied two ponies, a pretty little black gelding called Moonshine and a lovely chestnut stallion named Golden Prince. After much begging and pleading my mother gave in and so both ponies travelled to Jersey on the ferry. It was a rough passage. I was sick as a dog! In due course, Moonshine was sold to a Guernsey family. Golden Prince, who fathered a foal with Cindy, was sold locally but we kept the foal 'Here's Harry' who became Angie's mount. Angela Binet, who lived up the road, and I had become best friends, and she was like a sister to me. The three of us, Angie, Philip and I, had many years of fun and adventure, galloping through the fields, jumping over hedges and playing cowboys and Indians in Green Rock Canyon, at the top of the bumpy lane, where the spooky German bunker was well camouflaged in the hedgerow.

Philip used to spend a lot of time with me. One day I was rolling the newly sown grass field with Prince, and Philip was sitting on the five-foot horse-drawn concrete roller next to me. We were returning home and had to make a sharp turn left in order to get onto the road. I misjudged the turn and the roller veered up the embankment. Philip fell off directly under the roller, which then came back down with such a bang and wallop. Thank God he just had a grazed cheek—it could have been fatal. It scared the living daylights out of me and I was most unpopular with Anne, my sister and Philip's mother!

When show time came around, I used to tie a long piece of string to my big toe and thread it through the window of my bedroom, which was upstairs on the second floor, and down to the front garden. Angie would get up at 5.00 am and come and pull the string to wake me up, so we could prepare the ponies for the show in St Helier, five miles away. There were no horse floats in those days—at least, we didn't have one. The reason I couldn't wake up with an alarm was that I used to have dreadful, scary nightmares and would take a long time to go to sleep. Once asleep, it was difficult to wake up. The nightmares were so vivid that many a night I'd sleep on a camp bed in Mum and Dad's dressing room, to be closer to them.

I used to catch the No. 3 bus to go to Jersey High School in St Helier. The girls from the Arsenal (public housing subsidised by the Parish) enjoyed bullying me and teasing me about my long hair worn in plaits. One day I retaliated and came off the worse for wear. I asked Mum and Dad for a bicycle to avoid having to take the bus. I was thrilled to be given a shiny new blue bike, which I took great delight in riding the five miles to school. However, on the way home I had to push it up St Saviour's Hill, which was too steep to ride. The boys from St Saviour's School were a rough lot. They were supposed to put their energies into learning crafts such as woodwork, as they hadn't passed their 11+ (an examination administered to English students in their last year of primary education). However, they delighted in pulling my plaits and teasing me, which I found quite frightening. So, bike riding was another short-lived venture.

Meanwhile, life continued as normal on the farm, where I felt safe and happy. As a child, I formed close bonds with the regular seasonal workers. I particularly remember Melanie, the wife of the head of a French family who came to Jersey every potato season to dig and pack the new potatoes. She was a wonderful woman who worked like a drover's dog. The family slept in the outhouse and used to smoke huge legs of ham in their enormous fireplace. Coming from Brittany, Melanie used to bring stacks of crepes which she'd made at home in a special pan before coming to Jersey. I used to steal one or two on a regular basis. They were totally irresistible. Poor Melanie, I don't know if she knew, but if she did, she didn't tell on me.

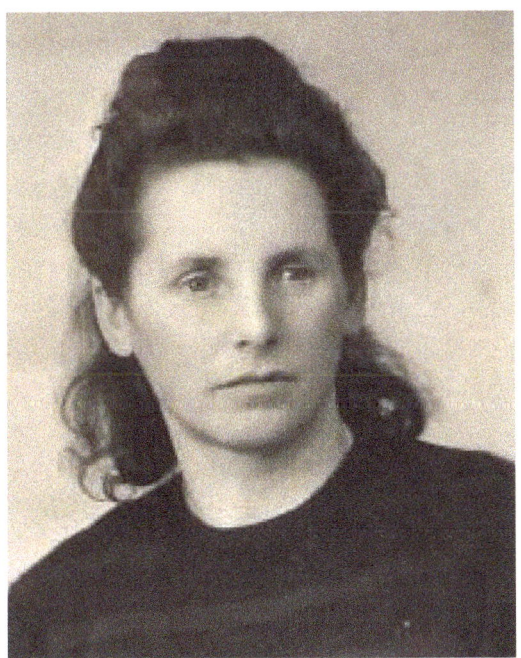

Melanie

The cottage

Yvonne Le Sueur and Elizabeth (right) dancing
'Les Geraniums' in Breton costume (1958 Jersey Eisteddfod)

We used to keep rabbits in hutches near the chickens. It was Grandpa Billot's job to walk the hedgerows and gather rabbit food. I couldn't bring myself to eating Mum's rabbit stew, nor veal which Dad had killed. It was the practice to knock newborn male calves on the head, skin them, then take them to Gerald Durrell's Zoo for the lions to eat. Male calves, unless specifically bred, were surplus to requirements. I still can't eat veal to this day.

During our busy lives, my family found time to go shrimping at St Catherine's Bay. Grandpa Billot had a large T-shaped net that he would trawl along the seabed in order to catch shrimp.

Mum, cousin Doris, Grandpa Billot

There are forty-foot tides in Jersey so it was important to fish at the right time. At low tide, we used to walk along the sand looking for 'key holes' made by razor fish. Once we found one, we'd trick the razor fish into popping up by putting a little salt down the hole. This made them believe the tide was coming in and therefore it was time to feed. Razor fish were a kind of sea slug wedged between two-by-ten centimetre shells, giving them the appearance of the old cut-throat razor, which the men in my family used to shave. Once caught, the fish were pickled in vinegar. I was not fond of eating them but enjoyed trying to catch them. We also went winkling, picking choice black winkles from the rocks and under the seaweed. I have fond memories of picking the winkle out of its shell, once cooked, with a large needle and eating it with fresh bread and butter.

Mum used to buy bags of dough from the baker in St Helier and bake copious amounts of fruit cake, which we'd take to the fields for the workers to wash down with our homemade cider.

We had an enormous cellar, complete with French casks. Prince used to walk round and round the cider press (a circular granite trough which contained a huge granite wheel) to which he was attached by a shaft. The special cider apples were grown in our orchard and placed in the press when ripe. It was my job, together with the choir boys from St Martin's Church, to bottle and cork the cider after fermentation. I remember one year we all got sozzled—that was the end of our cider making!

In 1959, at eleven years of age, I was beginning to mature. I decided I wanted my long chestnut hair cut—I could almost sit on it. Bath time was a torment. Mum used to put the galvanised tin bath in front of the Aga in the kitchen for warmth. She used to boil huge vats of water and then pour them into the bath. This was a Friday night ritual and I was the lucky first of three to share the bath. The agony came after, when Mum used to brush and comb my hair. Because my long hair had been in plaits all week, it was frizzy—there was no such thing as conditioner. The other days of the week we used to wash in our bedrooms, containing washstands, pitchers, bowls and face cloths. We had no running water and the loo was up the back garden path in a little wooden house. At night we used potties under our beds.

Elizabeth before haircut

Chapter 1 1940–1945

Chapter 2
1960-1968

In 1960, when I was twelve years of age, my parents retired from farming and moved from La Ville Bree to La Chasse Cottage, St Martin, which Dad had inherited from his Mother. Mum allowed me to choose the wine-coloured carpet and the whole place was redecorated. It was wonderful to live in a home with modern conveniences. Hot and cold water in the kitchen and bathroom, which housed not one but two flushing toilets! We were able to keep my horses in a purpose-built stable. I didn't realise then how lucky I was. It must have been an expensive project. Dad had three fields, one in front of the house, one beside the house and one at the top of St Catherine's Hill. The field at the top of St Catherine's Hill was to have a great influence on my life.

La Chasse Cottage

Dad had been part of the Honorary Police serving as a centenier of the Parish of St Martin. Each parish in Jersey elects members of the Honorary Police, who assist the connétable of the parish to maintain law and order. I remember the election being held for the Constable (Le Connétable de la Paroisse de St Martin) when we were at La Ville Bree. Dad was president of the Rozel Rovers Football Club, and his team, who also had a band, barracked for him during the election by performing on the back of our lorry in the front garden. I vividly remember, *Oh when the saints, Oh when the saints, Oh when the saints come marching in*. Dad had the support of the community and won by a landslide. He carried on the tradition set by his father and grandfather. Their impressive photos hang to this day on the walls in the Parish Hall. Unfortunately, that family tradition ends there, as Dad had no sons to take up the mantle. The community appreciated Dad's great service to the parish over thirty-three years and honoured him with a handmade solid silver candelabra and a wallet presented at the parish dinner and dance, held at Hotel de France in his honour. He was regarded as a compassionate but firm Chief of Police and Mayor and was sorely missed after he relinquished his duties.

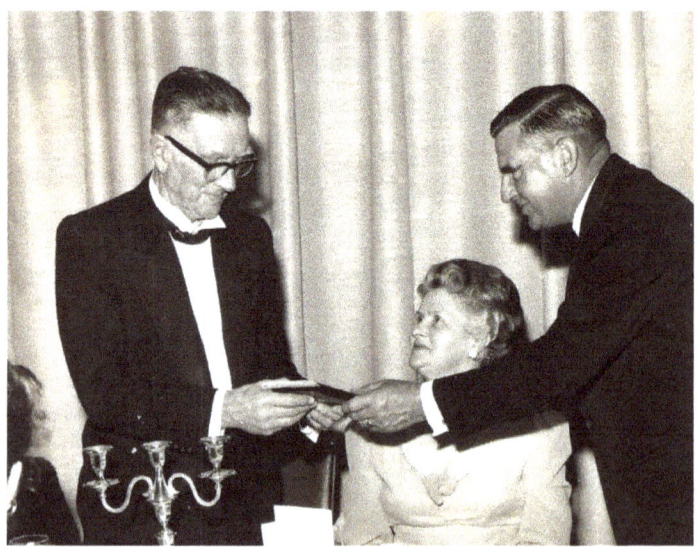

Dad (left) being presented with a hand-made silver candelabra and wallet at the parish dinner; Mum and George Le Masurier

Dad

One day, in my thirteenth year, I was hoeing the potatoes that had been planted in the field at the top of St Catherine's Hill. It was chance that I happened to be there that day, as I didn't normally do that kind of work. A tractor came along with a blond, shirtless Adonis at the wheel. My heart went aflutter and I remember thinking *I want to marry that man!* I had never been interested in the opposite sex before, but something stirred within me. I managed a few glances and I saw that he was looking at me. At that stage I didn't know who he was or where he came from.

After school and on weekends, I rode my pony down to St Catherine's Bay and swam him in the cool waters. Strangely enough, Adonis used to lead his farm horse from the meadow across the road back to his home, Waverley Farm, and I would see him on my return from the bay. We would exchange a look and a smile but it took quite some time before he plucked up the courage to talk to me. He later told me that he would watch and wait for me. Ian Jack Larbalestier became my first boyfriend and the only love of my life. He was born on 11 March 1943, making him five years my senior.

Waverley Farm

During the early days of our courtship, Ian Larbalestier morphed into Ian Larbalestier Kempster. He made the decision to change his name by deed poll in gratitude to the Kempsters for bringing him up. His father Bernard Larbalestier and his uncle John had drowned when trying to escape from Jersey to England (to enlist in the Armed Forces) in a little rowboat in the middle of the night, during the German occupation.

The following extract quotes Roy Thomas in *Lest We Forget*, a book specifically written about the escapes and attempted escapes from Jersey during the German occupation.

One Came Back ...

An entry in Leslie Sinel's Occupation Diary for 29 November 1944 reads:

Two more have drowned while attempting to escape. A German notice states that during the night of November 27–28 three young men tried to get to France in a boat they had obtained by false pretences; it drifted and was thrown against the cliffs; two were drowned and the third now awaits punishment.

It is only in recent times that the full story of this tragic failure has come to light from the survivor and only eye-witness, Peter Noel.

Bernard Larbalestier, aged 28 at the time, and his brother John, four years younger, ran the family pharmaceutical business in Charing Cross, St. Helier; nearby was a show room of J.W. Huelin Ltd. where Peter Noel was employed and it was through this working proximity that they became friendly.

Following the D-Day landing in June 1944, thoughts of attempting an escape developed into enthusiastic discussion between John and Peter, who were both of the same age; an initial scheme of trying to build their own craft was soon dismissed owing to the chronic shortage of suitable materials, but, through the pharmacy business, John heard of a local doctor who owned a 2-seater Folboat (like assault boats, this two seater canoe can be folded flat. It was designed to fit through a submarine hatch). Although reluctant at first to sell, the doctor eventually agreed to part with the Folboat for eighty pounds. The canoe, in its canvas cover plus an outboard motor were safely moved from a garage in St Clement's Road, on the edge of town, to the rear of the Larbalestier's shop in Charing Cross.

A friend of Peter's who worked at Huelin's, Len Murphy, was a fisherman in happier times and he advised Peter of a suitable embarkation point in the north east of the island, a path which led over a cliff in the Beauvallet area of Rozel and down to the sea, where the Folboat could be hidden in a niche in the rocks; despite having to avoid the anti-personnel mines sewn along the cliff edge, this part of the operation was carried out without incident. On the day of departure—sometime in July/August, having left their bicycles at a nearby farm, they made their way down the cliff path, again avoiding the mines and the barbed wire which was strewn about, assembled the Folboat, waited until it was dark and then set off, paddling two or three miles out due north before they fitted the engine on and attempted to start it; this it refused to do, despite the fact that it had been tested beforehand. Neither John nor Peter felt physically capable of paddling to France, so all they could do was return to the island; the Folboat drifted to the east, and at about 3.00 a.m. they landed west of La Coupe, sinking the craft and its contents, which included a batch of letters from fellow islanders written to relatives in England. They then crossed the rocks towards Rozel Bay and at about 7.00 a.m. they reached the main road, collected their bicycles from the farm and returned to St Helier.

Despite this setback, their enthusiasm to escape remained and John's brother Bernard then indicated his wish to join them in another attempt.

It came to be known that a number of small boats were stored in premises next to Norman's warehouse in Commercial Buildings; the Larbalestiers knew Arthur Norman well enough to ask him whether he could persuade the owner of the adjacent store to "look the other way", whilst a boat was quietly removed; this operation was successfully undertaken through the help of a friendly driver and his charcoal-driven covered van. The boat—12ft long—was transported into the town area from the Commercial Buildings to a carpenter by name of Hedouin who had a workshop in Le Geyt Street, St Helier where it was prepared for sea.

Peter Noel, the sole survivor. Photograph reproduced from Lest We Forget *by Roy Thomas*

John heard of a farmer in St. Martin who had stored away a small Seagull outboard motor, which he sold for twenty five pounds; this engine was brought back to town in a home-made box on wheels trailer behind a bicycle and taken to the rear of the Charing Cross premises where it was tested and found to be operating satisfactorily.

Bernard made contact with Mr. Bertram from "Bellair" Fauvic and it was agreed for them to leave from there. The boat and occupants moved to Fauvic in the same lorry without incident on the day of departure—27 November, 1944.

The three young men rested up in a small building to the rear of "Bellair" to await nightfall; at that time, it was a mild night with a little mist.

A significant event occurred during this waiting period, when an employee of Mr. Bertram, who lived in the small building, tried to persuade the trio to abandon their attempt, saying that the weather was going to change quickly and that they would be foolish to attempt a crossing. However, enthusiasm over-ruled the wise head and sometime between 10 and 11 p.m. they moved the boat down to the sea, loaded up and were off.

They rowed out for about 3–4 miles before they

started the engine which functioned for some 15–20 minutes before the throttle cable parted, due probably to years of non-use; they had no tools or spares to effect repairs and, to make matters worse, the weather changed—the wind increased from the south-east and drove them back in increasingly rough seas towards St. Catherine's breakwater—the warning of a few hours before by an unknown person was coming true. They jettisoned the useless engine and awaited their fate.

As luck would have it, they were swept to the south and innerside of the breakwater; as the boat hit the breakwater, Peter managed to jump out and cling on to the rough side of the granite and climbed up to the top. Here he looked back down; John was in the water with an inflated car inner-tube around him, while Bernard was astride the stricken boat, which had overturned.

Peter called down to them, and said he would try and find some rope; he discovered a length of wire, about 25–30 ft long, on the breakwater, passed it over the wall down to John—Bernard looked reasonably safe for the moment—with the intention of pulling John back down the breakwater until he could climb up in safety.

Just before reaching this spot, Peter, still pulling John, came across a massive barbed-wire entanglement right across the breakwater; here, Peter had no alternative other than to climb down the wall, pass under the obstruction and climb up the other side; this he succeeded in doing, but when he took up the strain to continue pulling, there was no resistance and John had gone—exposure and exhaustion had taken its toll.

Although greatly shocked at this, Peter immediately set about returning to the end of the breakwater to check on Bernard; before climbing under the wire again, he saw a notice 'Achtung Minen' on the land-side of the obstruction! Luckily, in his movements on the breakwater, he had only walked on the wide granite edge of the breakwater and not ventured on to the main part. He walked back to the end of the breakwater where he found the upturned boat, but no Bernard, so obviously he had succumbed to the cold and tempestuous seas.

By now it was about 3 a.m. Peter went back down the breakwater again, under the wire, on to the main road. There was a small building located there and across the road was another wire obstacle—and a German sentry. Quite clearly the game was up and

Peter was taken into a building nearby which was used as a guardhouse and housed an officer and six or so men.

St Catherine's Breakwater

At 7 a.m. he was taken to the Weighbridge in St. Helier, where he was questioned for ten hours; later that day he was transferred to the German wing of the Gloucester Street prison; two weeks later he was sentenced by Court Martial to ten months in prison for "attempted espionage." He remained in custody until Liberation Day on 8th May, 1945.

During his sojourn in Gloucester Street he met up with many locals who were serving various terms of incarceration and a form of "illuminated scroll" containing the names of many of the political prisoners was designed and organised by Peter and presented, during that time, to the prison chaplain, Rev. Quarrie.

Postscript

The body of John Larbalestier was found near St. Catherine and at an inquiry held on 29 December 1944, an open verdict was returned. The funeral service was held two days later at St. Simon's Church. The body of his brother Bernard was never recovered. They are commemorated in a tapestry in the Jersey Maritime Museum.

Ian's English mother, Jacqueline Whimperis, I was told was unable to look after him because she had to work. Arthur and Micheline Kempster, who were childless and friends of Bernard, were delighted to have Ian and treated him as their own. Although Jacqueline was to marry Harry Swanson after the war and would try desperately to get Ian back, he didn't want to leave the Kempsters and would have nothing to do with his mother. I only know what Ian told me of his childhood, and he was reticent to speak of it in detail.

I was the envy of my friends because my boyfriend

used to take me to and pick me up from school in his flashy Sunbeam Alpine sportscar.

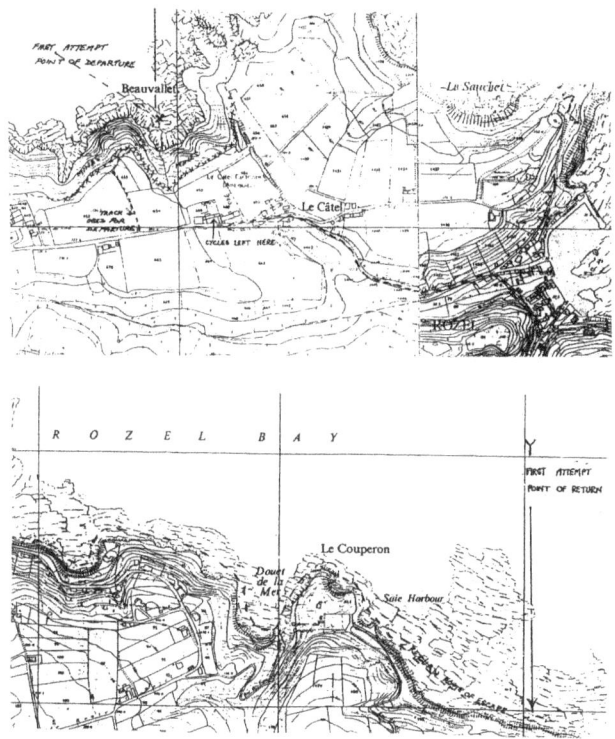

Map by Peter Noel showing the route through the minefield to the point of departure X, the subsequent landing place Y and the return to where Peter and John had left their bicycles

Page from Roy Thomas's book Lest We forget

A recent photograph taken at low tide and in calm weather illustrates the approximate positions of impact (A), where Peter lost contact with John (B), and where the up-turned boat was found (C).

Page from Roy Thomas's book Lest We forget

Ian in Sunbeam Alpine

He treated me to my first car, an old convertible MG, complete with running boards. One day in the rain I drove around a slippery, leaf littered bend and crashed into a brick wall. The poor old fragile car, frame made of wood, just collapsed in a heap!

My next car, courtesy of Ian, was a white convertible Triumph Spitfire, which I used to drive to attend Henrietta Nickels Secretarial College, after finishing high school.

Elizabeth in 1930s MG sports car

Elizabeth in Triumph Spitfire

When going out with Ian, I noticed that he always had a bottle of rum under the seat of his car. I didn't pay much attention to it at first, but when he enrolled in a hotel management course at Hendon College in London and spent a lot of his time in the pub, I began to wonder if he was tiring of me or whether he was liking alcohol a bit too much. I spent a month with him in London before returning home to start looking for my first job.

On his graduation Ian was employed as manager of Les Arches in Jersey, an upmarket hotel venue, engaging top pop music bands from England. After visiting me at night he would return to Les Arches and become embroiled in the nightlife. He began lying about how much time was spent at Les Arches, which was to become his second home, so I felt I could no longer trust him.

I decided to spread my wings both from home and Ian and rented a flat in Mont Millais, which I shared with Gina, my boxer dog. I started my first job after graduation from secretarial college, as a receptionist/telephonist at the Grand Hotel and also modelled for a friend who was a student photographer.

Elizabeth at sixteen years of age

As the Triumph was being troublesome, I decided to sell it and replaced it with an RGS Atalanta (a British racing-green racing car which had no roof but an Aston Martin engine). It was a purpose-built car for racing at Silverstone, England—unlikely to appeal to the mass buyer. The salesman must have rubbed his hands with glee when my enthusiasm overtook my common sense and I drove out of the second-hand car sales garage in my new acquisition!

RGS Atalanta with Gina behind the wheel

I wanted to be free so decided I would drive through France and Spain, finishing in Lisbon, Portugal. I left Gina with Mum and Dad, handed in my notice, put the car on the ferry to Dinard, and off I went. I almost got to the south of France when the inevitable happened—the car broke down. I arranged to have it shipped back to Jersey, at poor Mum and Dad's expense. I then carried on to Lisbon by coach and train. I decided to go to the British Embassy and ask for a job. I was extremely fortunate to be at the right place at the right time, because there was a clerical position vacant.

Elizabeth and Mum at the British Embassy in Lisbon, Portugal, 1967

I boarded at the home of a funny little old lady. Her name was Nelly and she continually fed me cabbage soup and potatoes, which made me fat. I made friends with some locals who spoke English and started going out with a handsome, well-to-do Portuguese man, who drove a Porsche. He used to rally drive and allowed me to have a go. I did very well but was over-confident and, when driving home around a roundabout, too fast, I crashed into a light pole.

This happened six months into my Portuguese adventure. I remember waking up in the ambulance with a nice man holding my hand. I acknowledged him with a smile and then found myself travelling down a long white and overwhelmingly bright tunnel. At the end there was an enormous loving enveloping warm light. I knew that I would either pass on or return to the living. It was an enlightening experience.

As I had been pinned against the steering wheel, I suffered a crushed chest, abrasions to my knees and a broken jaw in two places, knocking out my front teeth. Luckily my boyfriend was unhurt but the car was a write-off. I was given a tracheotomy to breathe and when deemed well enough to travel I was sent to St Bartholomew's in London for further treatment. My jaws were wired together for quite some time. Dad flew over to see me and so did Ian, who told me that was the last of my gallivanting around. He would marry me.

After my recovery I returned to Jersey and began making preparations for our wedding. As a child I used to help stook the hay in the meadow. One day I had watched a small plane fly overhead and thought, *I wish I could fly*. Well, Ian had the same ambition so we decided to get our private pilot's licences before the wedding.

Elizabeth stooking hay in meadow at a very young age, when she had her first thoughts of learning to fly

My first lesson in a Cessna 150 was as 'pilot under training' and we flew from Jersey to Guernsey and back. Unfortunately, due to lack of time and inclement weather, we were unable to obtain our licences after completing thirty-one hours under instruction and thirty minutes solo. I was to rectify this at a later stage.

Elizabeth and flying instructors

On 15 April 1968 Ian and I married in St Martin's Church. It was a beautiful spring day and after the church ceremony we were transported by horse and carriage to Hotel de France where we were splendidly waited on by the staff. Our 200 guests had a good time, I believe.

Ian had told me that he always wanted to go to Australia, so a few days after we were married we flew to Sydney at the invitation of the Australian Government as 'Ten Pound Poms'. Ten Pound Pom is a colloquial term used to describe the British citizens who migrated to Australia as a part of the Assisted Passage Migration Scheme after the Second World War—migrants paid a ten pound processing fee. Being young, adventurous and newly married, I was keen to go with him though I did not think it would be a lifelong change.

Mr. Peter George Dorey Kempster and Miss Anne Rose Mary Barry.

Mr. Ian Larbalestier Kempster and Miss Elizabeth Eunice Billot.

JERSEY LIFE

Kempster-Billot

After their marriage ceremony at St. Martin's Parish Church on Easter Monday, Mr. and Mrs. I. L. Kempster drove to their reception at the Hotel de France in a carriage and pair with Mr. C. Le Breton as coachman. The bride was 19 year old Elizabeth Eunice Billot, daughter of the Constable of St. Martin and Mrs. T. G. Billot, while the groom, Mr. Ian Larbalestier Kempster, is the son of Mrs. A. M. J. Kempster of The Cottage, Waverley Farm, St. Martin.

The bride was given away by her father and she was attended by her nieces Sarah Perchard and Marjorie Lacey, and the bridegroom's second cousins, Sarah Griffin and little Paul Kempster, and her matron of honour was Mrs. G. Meyer. The bride had a full length white dress of shot silk with a long train and her headdress was in the shape of a hood. She carried a bouquet of orchids. The bridesmaids' dresses were also long princess-line in delicate primrose yellow and they carried baskets of flowers. The best man was Mr. David Kempster, cousin of the groom.

At the reception at the Hotel de France, the 200 friends and relations learned of the couple's forthcoming journey to Australia where they hope to take up farming.

Rand-Vautier

The wedding took place recently at Eden Chapel, Maufant, of Mr. Ronald Leslie Rand, manager of West Park Pavilion, and Miss Maureen Antoinette Vautier.

Mr. Rand is the son of Mrs. E. Rand of Upper Lattimore Road, St. Albans, Herts, and of the late Mr. Rand, and the bride is the daughter of Mrs. A. G. Vautier, of Sunnydene, Maufant, and the late Mr. Vautier. The bride, who was given in marriage by her brother Mr. John Vautier, was attended by her niece, 4 year old Nina Raffray and 5 year old Sarah Louis Gothard, daughter of her employer. She wore a short white guipure lace dress with a matching hat, and the children wore dresses of fiesta pink satin with matching flowered bonnets and they carried baskets of flowers. The best man was Mr. John Stocker, a friend of the bridegroom.

The wedding reception was held for 70 guests at the Grand Hotel, following

WEDDINGS IN JERSEY

which Mr. and Mrs. Rand left for their honeymoon in Spain and Portugal.

Clapham-Le Roux

The wedding took place recently at St. Brelade Parish Church of Mr. Robin Patrick Clapham and Miss Jean Ann Le Roux.

The bride is the daughter of Mr. and Mrs. E. W. Le Roux of 4 Ocean View, Almorah, St. Helier and the groom is the younger son of Mrs. E. Clapham of 77 New Street, and the late Mr. A. H. Clapham.

The bride wore a full length dress in white Swiss Duchesses satin with a Victorian collar and flowing train of guipure lace. The bouquet was of arum lilies and blue hyacinth florets.

The bridesmaids were her sister Miss Barbara Le Roux and three friends. Their dresses were of forget-me-not blue terylene lawn, full length and trimmed with matching guipure lace on the sleeves.

The best man was Advocate M. H. Clapham, brother of the groom. The reception was at the Marina Grill, Portelet and the honeymoon was spent in London.

Kempster-Barry

The wedding took place recently at St. Mary and St. Peter's Roman Catholic Church, St. Helier, of Mr. Peter George Dorey Kempster and Miss Anne Rose Mary Barry.

The 20 year old bride is the daughter of Mr. and Mrs. W. P. Barry of 1 Beaulieu Park, St. Saviour's Road, and the groom, an assessing clerk at the States Income Tax Department, is the son of Mr. and Mrs. G. A. V. Kempster of Sheringham, Les Varines, St. Saviour. A friend and colleague of the bride—she is employed as an assistant librarian at the Public Library—was bridesmaid—Miss Patricia Bannier, while a brother of the groom, Mr. John Kempster was best man.

The bride, who was given in marriage by her father, wore a full length gown of white satin with white lace overlay and with a matching head-dress. She carried a bouquet of white hyacinths. The bridesmaid wore a full length empire line dress of fuchsia pink peaue de soie, with a matching jacket trimmed with pink daisies. Her bouquet comprised blue hyacinths, white double freesias and pink carnations. The honeymoon was spent in London.

Cutting from Jersey newspaper, 1968

Elizabeth and Ian's wedding, 1968

Chapter 3
1968-1970

On 18 April 1968, we said farewell to our families and boarded a British United plane to London, then a connecting flight to Sydney.

We bought an ex-naval short wheel base, baby blue Land Rover, named Bluebell, and set off on our travels. We intended seeing most of Australia before deciding where to settle.

Following our map along the Snowy River Mountain scheme we found a lovely isolated spot in a valley off the road. I remember thinking we hadn't gone far on the map for a day's driving. The landscape was totally foreign—strangely shaped trees where the leaves hung vertically and the trunk colours varied from white to pink and all shades in between. The topography was different too. I realised coming from a tiny insular island to such a vast open island with seemingly never-ending horizons was going to be an eye-opener. We had bought a little camping gear to cook with and sleeping bags to sleep in the back of the vehicle.

Elizabeth and Ian's plane to London

Bluebell

Ian

We were preparing our evening meal when the sun started falling out of the sky—no twilight here—when suddenly there was maniacal laughter echoing up and down the valley. I was startled. I told Ian, 'I think there must be wild natives here'. We hightailed out of there at a rate of knots only to learn, much later, that it was the kookaburras' habit to settle themselves before bedtime and let all the other birds know of their whereabouts with their raucous song!

We continued on our journey up north, taking in the view around Swansea. This was the end of April. We saw some Jerseys, a familiar sight, just outside Tenterfield. We then headed for the coast at Byron Bay and drove through Coolangatta and Southport to Brisbane. The coastline had been decimated by a cyclone and other extreme weather events the previous year, so the Gold Coast was not what we had envisioned.

I was struck by the style of the houses—differently shaped, made of timber and galvanised iron roofing. These were sitting on top of stilts and varied in size from tiny cottages to large, elegant homes surrounded by verandahs. I came to understand the reason for this 'Queensland' design which compensated for the weather extremes of heat and flooding rains.

We decided to head west of Brisbane, along the Warrego Highway, passing through Ipswich, Toowoomba, Chinchilla, Roma, Mitchell and Charleville. We headed north from Charleville through Augathella, Tambo, Blackall, Barcaldine, Longreach and Winton. The further north we went, the more sparse the vegetation became. There seemed to be miles upon miles of flat dry land, with no sign of stock. Between Winton and Kynuna we spied a green cloud coming towards us. This massive flock of wild budgerigars appeared to be racing Bluebell. It was a wonderful sight, having seen only caged birds, treated as pets. I had never imagined budgerigars being free and flying in such large flocks. They twisted and turned, changing different shades of green as they went—marvellous. I wondered what they lived on as there wasn't a blade of grass, vegetation or trees to be seen.

We overnighted in Kynuna in what was supposed to be a hotel. The room had hessian bags for walls and a double bed which we shared with gidgee bugs—millions of them. They are also known as stink beetles. I couldn't stand them crawling all over me, so we left and carried on driving. By this time, we had had enough exploring and when we got to Cloncurry, we treated ourselves to a hot shower and decent bed in a motel.

We decided to have dinner in a pub and whilst there we met an agricultural representative. We asked if he knew of any jobs in the area and he replied that he did. We began work at Fort Constantine, just north of Cloncurry, which was owned by Stanbroke Pastoral Company. Kevin Shaw was the general manager and used to fly around their various properties. Ian was the cowboy and I was the housemaid. Being a cowboy entailed getting up at 4.00 am, finding the night horse and riding out in the unknown to bring in the milking cows in the dark. Ian had never milked a cow before, so I taught him. Having been brought up on a dairy farm, I was accustomed to hand milking from an early age. Ian and I used to tie the cows' back legs with a rope to a post. They were not quiet dairy cows but half wild station shorthorns. We lived in a one bedroom portable hut which had louvres all around and a toilet adjoining.

Ian outside our little home at Fort Constantine, Cloncurry

Daniel *Jersey potatoes*

We decided to buy a black Great Dane puppy named Daniel for company—not a wise choice for a number of reasons! He outgrew our vehicle and eventually we had to re-home him. Ian was able to grow some Jersey Royal potatoes and Jersey tomatoes—a little reminder of home. There weren't the stringent Australian Customs biosecurity restrictions that are in place today.

We ate in the communal dining room, having all our meals supplied. Ian was given the opportunity to join the mustering camp as camp cook. I was keen to join in but the head stockman told me they didn't have any spare saddles! That was his way of saying 'No women in the camp'. My response was, 'I'll ride bareback!' They were to take two days to drive the cattle into Cloncurry, but being an all-male team, I was allowed to accompany them for half a day's muster only. I was told when we reached the halfway point and then had to retrace my steps back to the homestead. Boy, did I have a sore bottom! Riding bareback for mile upon mile made me wish I had never volunteered. I wouldn't give the men the pleasure of saying 'I told you so' on their return, so I simply suffered in silence.

Ian

Elizabeth and stockman

When the team returned without Ian I became extremely worried. The head stockman told me that Ian had got drunk in the pub and, after ringing the church bell, had 'gone off with a gin'. I didn't know what he meant. I was beside myself with worry and anger. Ian eventually turned up with the camp belongings in tow and, boy, did I let him have it! The men had a good laugh at my expense. I had my first lesson in Aussie sense of humour.

After three months at Fort Constantine we decided to continue exploring. We planned to drive north to Normanton and marked our journey on our Shell roadmap, intending to head east to Cairns, south to Townsville and then back west, passing through Cloncurry on our way to the Stuart Highway via Mt Isa, Camooweal and Tennant Creek.

By the time we reached Normanton I was very ill, not able to eat or drink—a cup of tea would result in vomiting. I was certain I had cancer. It was a growth all right, not the dreaded 'C' word but the 'P' word. We were thrilled to learn I was expecting but I feared the long, overland journey to Perth, which was our next destination. We retraced our steps back to Cloncurry and then headed west to Tennant Creek. I just had to lie down across the front seats with my head on Ian's lap through Alice Springs and Coober Pedy, before ending our drive at Kingoonya. I was so sorry not to enjoy the trip. Even the sight of opals couldn't put a smile on my face.

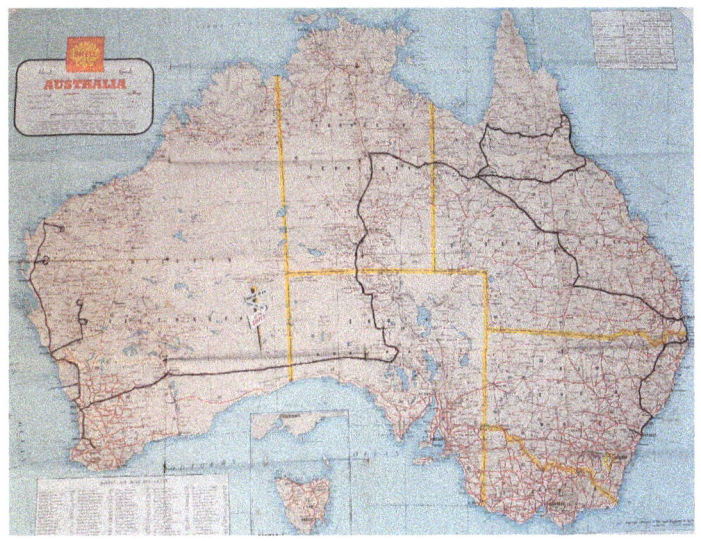

Our travels across Australia marked on map from Sydney, Brisbane, Cloncurry, Normanton back down to Tennant Creek, Kingoonya, across the Nullarbor to Perth, on our honeymoon

When checking into the pub at Kingoonya I thought we were in the wild west. A small wiry man burst out of the pub swing doors chased by a large well-endowed woman brandishing a straw broom. I don't know whether or not she caught him. That *did* put a smile on my face.

We caught the train from Kingoonya to Kalgoorlie,

freighting the Land Rover and Daniel in the goods section of the train. I had a distant cousin in Perth so the attraction was to be in the company of someone from Jersey. I really missed my mother, feeling the need to talk to her about childbirth. She had never spoken about the experience. I think she didn't want to frighten me off, after her bad experiences.

We arrived in Kalgoorlie on 13 October 1968 and headed off to Perth. We were shocked to learn the following morning that a strong earthquake, magnitude 6.5 with an epicentre at Meckering, injured at least seventeen people and caused extensive property and road damage. The road we had driven on from Kalgoorlie had huge chasms and was now impassable.

We stayed with Yvonne and Tom Pullinger in Clermont. Yvonne (nee Perchard) was Dad's first cousin. Her father, being the eldest son, had inherited La Chasse which my great grandfather had built. This was supposed to ensure the property stayed within the family. The eldest son got the prize possession, whilst the others shared the remainder. Unfortunately, the curse of alcohol dependency took its toll on Yvonne's father and the main house was sold, but fortunately the cottage was inherited by his sister, Grandma Billot, and was then passed on to Dad.

We traded Bluebell in and bought a new Ford station wagon. We looked at farms for sale in the south-west and decided on Lukin Springs at Boyup Brook. It was a nice little mixed farming property, running a few thousand sheep, a couple of hundred head of cattle and was only five miles out from Boyup Brook.

Our first new car in Australia, a ford station wagon

Lukin Springs, Boyup Brook, WA

We arranged to have all our furniture shipped over from Jersey by sea container, an expensive but worthwhile exercise. We managed to cram it all into the cottage. It felt good to be surrounded by familiar furniture.

I also bought a Jersey cow, another comfort memory, and named her Design. I milked by hand every other day, set the milk in a large bowl in the fridge, then skimmed off the cream to make butter and cheese. My butter churn made the best butter and so tasty when salted.

As my pregnancy progressed I suffered from toxaemia and high blood pressure, so I was put into hospital in Perth for the final month. Dr Wilders decided to induce me on 15 May 1969. After a difficult labour, Zak Ian George was born at 6.10 pm, weighing 7 lb 7 oz. His head was so misshapen, due to the use of forceps, that I wondered whether he would be okay. He turned out to be a beautiful baby but suffered from severe colic for the first six months. He was putting on a lot of weight so I was told there was nothing wrong. I really missed my mother at this time.

Ian's cousin (by deed poll) Sue and her husband Alisdair Courtney (Deputy Head of Scotch College) in Perth, were Zak's godparents. He was christened at two months of age at the Anglican church in Boyup Brook.

We harvested Kondinin Rose clover for sale as seed. I remember getting so itchy when driving the harvester—it was a filthy job. Ian decided we needed a new shearing shed and so it was finished just before shearing time. It was a delight to work in and I learnt how to class wool. The shearers nearly went on strike because of my cooking, or I should say because of my lack of cooking skills. I knew how to cook liver stew, which I loved, as I had written to ask Mum for the recipe. However, continuous servings of liver stew went down like a lead balloon. Mrs Muriel Cross, who used to help me in the house and was a great cook, came to my rescue and gave me a crash course in basic cooking, which saved the day.

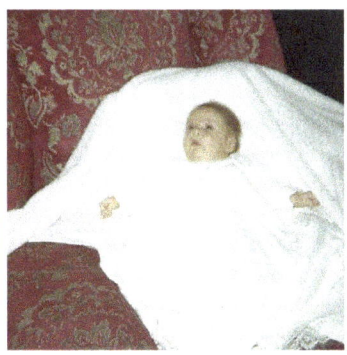

Zak (nine months)   *Zak's christening*

In the meantime, Ian decided he wanted a larger land holding and negotiated with Keith Smith, our next-door neighbour, to buy him out. Property prices were at a premium because wool was a pound per pound. He put Waverley Farm on the market together with office buildings and the parfumerie shop (inherited from the Larbalestiers) in St Helier. The reverse was true of the market in Jersey at that time, and we sold at giveaway prices. Within a year the wool market collapsed in Australia and we found we couldn't meet the repayments on the second property.

Unfortunately, we lost a great deal of money through the sale of the combined property in Australia, but kept a few thousand sheep which the new owner didn't want. Since the market had collapsed we trucked a couple of thousand sheep up to Dandaragan, just outside of Moora, where we agisted them until they were able to be sold.

Chapter 4
1971-1973

Ian was able to secure a position as caretaker on Mungedar Station, Dandaragan, and we lived in the outstation, Limestone Cottage, where I was able to buy and keep Tinkerbell, a palomino brood mare, Cherokee, a 12.2 hand skewbald pony mare and Monty, a little bay pony.

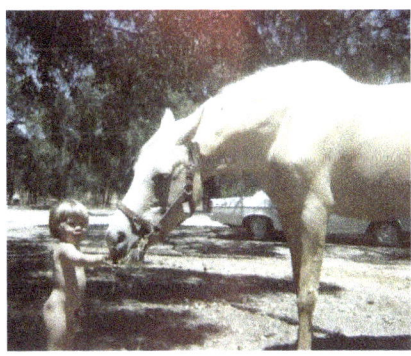

Zak (age eighteen months) and Tinkerbell

Zak (age three) on Cherokee

As I wanted a companion for Zak, close in age, I fell pregnant again. Though nauseous and unwell, fortunately I didn't suffer toxaemia or high blood pressure.

Warren Thomas was born on 7 November 1971, weighing 7 lb 2 oz. He was a delightful baby and there was no doubting who his father was. He was the spitting image of Ian as a baby, with his Persil white hair.

Ian had kept in touch with Pat and Keith Smith from Boyup Brook, so we asked if they would be godparents. Warren was christened at three weeks of age in the little Anglican church in Dandaragan.

Warren (one year)   *Pat and Keith Smith at Warren's Christening*

Mum and Dad came to visit us for Christmas in November 1972. They stayed until January 1973. I was so happy to see them. Zak was now three and a half years old and Warren was just one year old. Mum and Dad used to take the boys up to the henhouse to feed the chooks. I had a lovely turkey named Prudence who used to squat when anyone approached so she could be patted. Mum also took to feeding a galah and lorikeet—although wild, they became quite tame and would perch on her shoulder.

Left: Dad, Warren and chooks

Right: Mum feeding lorikeet and galah

We went to Greenhead, Jurien Bay, on holiday and stayed in the CWA cottage. It was very hot and dry. Mum found the heat very trying, but Dad revelled in the warmth. Dad had noticed that there were many empty bottles in the sheds and surrounds at Limestone Cottage. He tried to tell me that 'this is no place for you, my girl'. I immediately became defensive and told Dad, in no uncertain terms, that Ian didn't have a drinking problem. I was not prepared to consider the long-term consequences of being married to a heavy drinker and, naively, I thought *Love would cure all*!

Greenhead, Jurien Bay, early 1973
Left: Mum   *Right: Dad, Elizabeth, Warren, Grant and Ian (left to right)*

Whilst at Jurien Bay, we met with Pat and Keith Smith who had bought the local store. Keith offered Ian a job, which he took. We moved there in 1973 and stayed for the winter. We enjoyed night fishing and bought a beach rod each. More often than not we would bring home a feed of tailor, which moved in schools along inshore coastal waters, slicing through schools of bait fish with their razor-sharp teeth. It felt exciting to experience that tug on the line and to reel them in, sometimes with quite a fight.

Chapter 5
1974-1975
Station Life

In 1974 Ian applied for a position as trainee manager on Murgoo Station in the Murchison. It is a pastoral lease sheep station situated approximately 112 kilometres to the north of Yalgoo and 146 kilometres west of Cue. It consists of 402 960 acres of mainly saltbush plains and mulga country. It was owned by the Aitken Brothers from South Australia but was suffering from drought at the time. However, whilst there the rains came and came and came. The waters came up and penetrated our cottage. Fortunately, we had enough bricks to raise the furniture, escaping inundation of our prized possessions.

The cottage *Hanging out the washing*

Zak on homemade raft *Nanette*

Ian made the boys a raft out of a couple of empty drums. We had great fun trying to propel it and this activity helped to make light of the situation we found ourselves in. Nanette, our pet goat, was determined to stay amused. She jumped up on an outside table and proceeded to eat the washing! She was so bored with the rain that she got into as much mischief as possible.

Fortunately, we had enough supplies of flour,

potatoes, onions, tinned beans and peas to see us through.

The rains gave the Atkins Brothers the opportunity to sell. The country looked magnificent after all the rain. It never ceases to amaze me how the land can be bare and parched with not a blade of grass in sight, then be totally transformed within a week or two into verdant green pastures after torrential rain. They sold to the Seaman family who were owner/operators. Therefore, there was no need for the existing staff and so we were on the lookout for a new job.

Fortunately, a position was vacant for the Manager of Manfred Station, just one hundred kilometres north of Murgoo. We again packed the furniture and carted it in the back of a truck, together with the horses, and drove to Manfred.

Living there, we were in the middle of nowhere as we still had to drive 212 kilometres back past Murgoo to get to Yalgoo, on a dirt road, and then turn west for another 217 kilometres to get to Geraldton on a sealed road.

There was a party telephone line at Murgoo but nothing at Manfred. We were quite isolated but we didn't mind. Manfred homestead was a beautiful old stone building with large verandahs back and front. The gardens were enormous and I took great pleasure in watering them and bringing them back to life. There were a couple of very old date palms by the side of the house and the fruit from these was the best I have ever tasted. I had never really liked dates before but love them now.

I kept Stormy, my chestnut Anglo Arab stallion (progeny of Tinkerbell) and used him to put over Cherokee, the little skewbald mare bought in Dandaragan. I intended breeding children's ponies for my sons to ride. Monty, their little bay beginner pony, had been badly foundered, but the dry station country suited him. He was a cheeky little thing and would walk under a low tree to wipe the boys off his back when he decided he didn't want to be ridden anymore. But he had a beautiful nature—the boys could crawl all over, under and between his legs with no one getting hurt.

We bought a German shepherd pup from Brisbane and called him Sabre, after Ian's childhood dog. He turned out to be the most wonderful companion for the boys. They loved him and he, in turn, adored them. It amazed me how the boys would ride him like a little pony, and he took it all in his stride, never once showing any sign of aggression.

Whilst at Manfred, Cherokee had a bay colt foal who we named Manfred after the property. Zak progressed from Monty to Manfred after I had broken him with the help of the horse-breaker, and he turned out to be a super pony. Warren learned to ride Monty and got the best out of him. His little legs would work at ten-to-the-dozen kicking Monty to make him go.

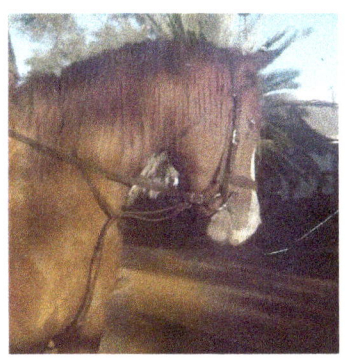

Stormy

Warren (age nine years) on Monty

As at Murgoo, we had only a thirty-two volt lighting plant. We used kerosene fridges and I had to wash by hand, although I would boil the sheets in the copper. Cooking was done in the cook house on a wood stove, which made the most beautiful bread, risen with Dribarm (dry yeast). I was quite happy to turn into a hippy.

Because of my watering, the gardens looked welcoming and cool. The semi-enclosed verandah at the back was covered in creepers. This attracted snakes and we kept plaited thick-gauge lengths of wire at strategic points around the homestead. I feared and hated snakes but learned to break their backs with a swing from the plaited wire. This immobilised them, making it easy to then kill them.

Zak and Warren shared a bedroom and one night, when checking them before retiring, I found a large brown snake in their room. I was terrified and quickly reached for a wire. As the boys were only six and four years old I didn't want to wake them. The snake was cornered and dangerous but somehow I managed to break its back without waking the boys!

Another scare happened when Zak got bitten by a yellow scorpion. I had read about deadly black scorpions in Africa and imagined the worst. Fortunately, the Australian ones are non-venomous but Zak did suffer an allergic reaction and his foot was swollen for quite a few days.

Ian's job was to check the windmills and troughs, so he'd be gone all day. The general manager, who ran the adjoining property, called in to see me one day. He apologised but said that he had to give Ian the sack. He had found empty bottles around the run. It was a dry station and so no alcohol was permitted. I was stunned, and unable to mentally process our dismissal. He said we should go to Geraldton to find other employment and could leave the furniture and horses there until we had somewhere to go.

Chapter 6
1976-1980

We went to Geraldton and had an interview for overseer of Wandagee Station, situated 125 kilometres north-east of Carnarvon, on the Minilya River. If I remember correctly, it comprised 250 000 square miles, ran 30 000 sheep and had approximately 500 wild cattle. There was a lovely old homestead with verandahs back and front.

Wandagee Station

Again, we had a thirty-two volt lighting plant and kerosene fridges. In summer the temperatures used to range from forty to fifty degrees Celsius in the shade. It was Zak's job, at seven years of age, to sweep the verandahs every day, much to his chagrin. Young and old sparrows used to drop dead, falling off the rafters, due to the extreme heat. It seemed we were back in drought conditions. We had to sleep on camp beds in the front garden as, being constructed of stone, the house was like an oven. Even then, we had difficulty sleeping, in a pool of sweat, particularly when continuous horizontal dry lightning lit up the horizon, hour after hour.

I had to cook for the men and ourselves as well as maintain the homestead. As Zak was due to start school I asked for assistance. Stockmen have huge appetites so the fortnightly mail run was eagerly awaited, bringing drums of dingo flour, Dribarm yeast, bags of potatoes, onions, cartons of tinned beans and peas and powdered milk. I tried establishing a veggie garden but the water was brackish and soon burnt any seedlings I had managed to coax to sprout from seed.

The terrain was mainly saltbush and Ian's job was to carry out daily windmill runs and ensure the pumps and miles of pipelines kept water in the troughs for the sheep. Because of the extreme heat, the men would have to kill a sheep every day. The following day the meat would turn green in the kerosene fridges. It was, however, the best hogget (two-tooth teenager—neither lamb nor mutton) I have ever tasted. Sheep grown on salt bush flats have a unique flavour.

The staff comprised 3–4 men who lived with their families in the camp, although they ate in the staff dining room. Penny, who had been brought up in a mission, helped me. She was a capable single woman in her forties and I appreciated her help. She cooked breakfast for the men and made their lunches. If a stockman had forgotten to hang his saddlebag on the peg in their dining room, she would not make lunch for him. She was a tough woman, missing her front teeth and would stand up to the men if they gave her cheek. I treated her as part of our family.

I used to bake two double loaves of bread daily. There's nothing like the wafting aroma of fresh bread coming out of the oven. A roast leg of hogget was also delicious and was something which we never tired of. It was usually devoured in a single sitting.

Penny and boys   *Penny*

It seemed at last that we had found somewhere to settle and where my children could feel at home. It was now time to teach. We enrolled in Carnarvon School of the Air and received the curriculum by mail. I would answer the roll call on the pedal radio at 7.00 am every day. Each station would be called in alphabetical order and, at my turn, I would answer, 'Good morning, Wandagee Station, over and out'. Zak's class would be called mid-morning and his teacher would follow the same procedure. It was difficult to conduct lessons on air and the majority of the teaching was done in the home classroom. Alfred Traeger, who invented the pedal radio, first introduced in Queensland in 1929, gave a voice to the bush and enabled John Flynn to create a 'mantle of safety' for the Royal Flying Doctor Service.

I thought that teaching my children would

be easy—little did I know! We had a designated classroom next to the kitchen and began lessons at 7.00 am after breakfast and everyone had gone to begin the day's work. *Dick and Dora* were a breeze and the maths part of the Cuisenaire rods were no problem. But Zak couldn't differentiate between colours. I suspected he was colour blind, but I was wrong. Poor Zak—I used to slap the ruler on my desk in frustration. I'm sure he was terrified. He eventually learned his colours and by the time he went to boarding school at twelve years of age, he was two years ahead of his peers in the classroom. We finished school at 12.00 pm, had lunch and then had a couple of hours to ourselves before having to start preparing the evening meal.

Warren started school two years later and, thank heavens, he didn't have 'colour' problems. He too was well ahead of his peers when he went to 'proper' school and was particularly good at advanced maths.

We were a tight-knit little family and enjoyed each others' company, apart from school time! During our couple of hours free time each day I taught the boys to ride horses. They were excellent horsemen and would practise gymkhana events for the Winning Pool Races, held annually, which was the highlight of the year. Zak on Manfred and Warren on Heidi (Cherokee's second foal) were nicknamed the two F-111s because of their speed and determination. Zak, being the older of the two, used to have the advantage but I admired Warren's gutsy performance in getting Heidi, who was very stubborn, to obey.

1977 Carnarvon School of Air. Zak and Warren front row, middle

Warren on Heidi   *Zak on Manfred with Sabre*

Both Zak and Warren won many ribbons. Zak was Champion Boy Rider, I was Champion Lady Rider and I also won the stockman's race, which was particularly pleasing, beating the young station hand guns.

Elizabeth on West Wind, a Wandagee Station thoroughbred that she trained for the winning Pool Races

As well as ponies, I was able to get two motorbikes, a Honda XR75 for Zak and a Yamaha Pee Wee 50 for Warren. The XR75 was a great, light, versatile bike but the Pee Wee 50 was a heavy little thing. The handlebars used to fold down and the rear mudguard was so close to the tyre that it kept clogging up with mud after rain. I was told it had been used to drop out of aircraft by parachute for military purposes. Poor little eight year old Warren persevered and eventually managed to control the machine without it falling over and pinning him to the ground.

Zak

Warren

Warren dressed as a chef

Speedy the racing car

Warren was always dressing up, using his imagination to create something out of nothing. We didn't have any dress up clothes or costumes on the station, and so he improvised with sheets, boxes, newspaper and whatever else he could find. He loved dressing up as a robber, in his dressing gown and fedora hat, or as a chef. He was a very imaginative and creative child.

As both Zak and Warren were growing up so quickly, I was longing to have more children. I had suffered a miscarriage but felt it would be okay to try again. I was lucky enough to fall pregnant and, apart from the usual morning sickness, I kept well.

And so, on 15 July 1978 I drove myself into Carnarvon, after advising the Royal Flying Doctor Service at 7.00 am on the pedal radio roll call, that I had begun labour. I was asked if I wanted the RFDS plane to come and collect me. I knew it wouldn't be a quick birth from my previous experiences. The Doctor, via the pedal radio, told me to take some delaying medication from the RFDS medicine chest, but I didn't—I didn't want to prolong the event! I left Zak and Warren at the station with Penny, as Ian had gone with the men for the day. It took one and a half hours along the dirt road to Minilya Roadhouse, then easy sailing down the sealed North Coastal Highway to Carnarvon for one hour, a total of 200 kilometres.

At 6.00 pm Ian Grant came into the world (weighing 7 lb) thanks to Dr Board and his staff at Carnarvon Hospital. 'Grant' as he came to be known, was a lovely baby and soon settled into a routine with big brothers to cart him around. I enquired about getting him christened and was very fortunate that retired Arch Bishop Muschamp of the Kalgoorlie Diocese (who happened to be in Carnarvon on holiday, relieving the current rector) was more than happy to make the long trip out to Wandagee Station to officiate at the ceremony. It was a lovely day and Grant, at six weeks of age, was extremely good. Keith and Edna Crooks from the Carnarvon RFDS base brought out the cake, which Edna had made and decorated. A number of neighbours made the journey and so Zak and Warren were able to play with their School of the Air classmates.

I asked Mrs Elliott, the wife of the station owner, to be godmother as Grant was born on her birthday. She flew up from Geraldton especially for the event. Jimmy Perchard, my nephew in Jersey, was also born on July 15th, so he became godfather. Keith Crooks stood in as local proxy.

Grant's christening
Top: Zak, Craig, friend, Edna Crooks, Warren, friend
Bottom left: Ian, Mrs Elliott, Grant, Elizabeth, Keith Crooks
Bottom right: The Bishop

The following day another annual event took place at our next-door neighbours'. It was Middalya Station's Shearing Shed Ball. What a night! Zak, as a pirate, and Warren, as a Roman soldier, entered in the fancy dress competition. Warren really played the part, jousting and threatening as he paraded around. He won first prize, and certainly deserved it.

Meanwhile Grant slept peacefully over the din in his bassinet on the wool bale scales!

Life returned to normal after a very exciting

couple of days. Station life was full-on but I loved it. There was no time for boredom—early to bed and early to rise was the routine. The boys led carefree lives outside on their bikes or ponies, with Sabre as their constant shadow and protector. Grant became part of the team, riding Monty, and he also had his own bike, sometimes giving Percy the Siamese a ride. Grant used to play policeman, chasing Warren who played the robber.

Middalya Station's Shearing Shed Ball. Warren (left), Zak (right)

Zak, Grant and Warren

Grant in coalscuttle

Grant on bike with cat

Grant chasing Warren

We worked seven days a week but Sundays were more relaxed and we could go for a drive with Ian in the Nissan ute. Ian, Grant and I were in the front with Zak and Warren hanging on the back with Sabre. We used to go treasure hunting for old bottles and glassware that had been left at campsites so long ago that they had morphed into beautifully coloured glass of all hues, shapes and sizes. We accumulated quite a collection. The other treasure we enjoyed digging up was in a dam that had been excavated but was still waiting for rain and run-off to fill it. We'd dig and find beautiful fossilised squid—they were the size of a little finger, shaped like torpedoes and opaque brown in colour. They were millions of years old and the remains of an inland sea. You could make out the spine when held up to the light.

We experienced a number of dust storms. It was so disheartening to have the homestead clean, only to find it coated in fine red dust by the end of the day. On one occasion the boys and I saw a huge cloud of red advancing towards the homestead. Accompanying it was a howling ferocious whirlwind. We watched in trepidation as what appeared to be a red tornado come towards the homestead and outbuildings. It blocked out the sky. It took all our strength to keep the kitchen windows shut. They were rattling so much I thought they were going to break as the winds tried to force them open. Then suddenly the twister shifted direction and followed the dip in the driveway down towards the huge brand new shed, which it picked up, twisted around, and dropped a quarter of a kilometre further on. It was as if the shed was made of paper instead of galvanised iron with concrete supports. The men came home to find such a mess.

Life on the station came with its unique challenges. We had a scare when Ian was syphoning petrol through a tube into a jerry can and was bitten in his mouth by a redback spider, which had been in the tube. Fortunately, it wasn't life-threatening but his mouth was swollen and sore for a number of days.

Snakes caused me a great deal of concern, far more than spiders. We had a sandpit around the side of the house in the shade, where the boys would play. I remember calling the boys in one day, and fifteen minutes later I went outside to get the washing in and found a death adder in the sandpit. I had another scare one day when, after sitting on the toilet, I got up and flushed it, dislodging a baby king brown snake that had been curled up under the bowl ledge. I nearly died of fright! It had crawled up through the outlet from outside to keep cool in the toilet. I immediately boiled a kettle of water and scalded the snake, which turned tail and retraced its route through the outlet outside, where the boys were waiting with a spade to do away with it. Needless to say, I always flushed the toilet and instructed everyone else to do the same before sitting down on the seat, even though the external pipe had been blocked after this incident!

There were no serious accidents out on the station but I once had to inject a stockman with morphine from the RFDS medicine chest while waiting for the RFDS plane to collect him because of a broken collarbone, sustained after falling off a horse. The poor man said his bottom felt like a pin cushion because of my clumsy attempts with the syringe. I didn't realise skin and tissue were so soft and my shaking hand kept jabbing him in and out.

Just before Grant's first birthday, a minor accident occurred. Warren was free-wheeling his bike down to the shed as the bicycle chain had come off and he was holding it across his handlebars, hoping Ian would fix it. The chain slipped and got caught in the front wheel spokes, cartwheeling Warren over the handlebars. It knocked him out and he had a number of cuts and bruises, but thankfully, he recovered after a little lie down.

A later incident occurred when Zak was riding his motorbike with Grant in front of him as a passenger. The story goes that Zak hit a tree as he was looking behind to see if the children from the stock camp were following. He fell off and Grant fell forward, breaking his nose. Grant would have only been about three or four years of age. Though it now seems young to be on a motorbike, that was normal practice on a station!

When Warren, aged perhaps nine years, was suffering with headaches and dizziness I was very concerned so I flew down to Perth with him to see a specialist. Fortunately, after tests, everything was okay but I now believe Warren was allergic to oleanders, which grew profusely around the perimeter of the homestead and are poisonous to stock.

In 1980 Mum and Dad celebrated their Golden Wedding Anniversary. We were delighted as a family to be able to fly back to Jersey for the event and spend three weeks catching up with everyone. I could see Dad was very frail and short of breath but Mum was a tower of strength and cared for him as she had always done.

From Australia we communicated with them by cassette tape as well as my weekly missive. We'd record one side, send it to Mum and Dad and they'd reply on the other side and send it back to us. They loved to hear our voices, and in particular those of the boys. Being bush kids, they told it as it was. We'd try to book a Christmas phone call from Carnarvon, but it wasn't always possible.

The Billot Family at Mum and Dad's golden wedding celebration

Elizabeth, Ruth, Dad, Mum, Anne, Mary (left to right) at Mum and Dad's golden wedding celebration

When we returned to Australia I became the proud owner of a new Super 8 movie camera, as

I wanted to record our daily lives. I used to take movies of life around the station, then send them to Perth for development, whereupon they'd return the spools, which were roughly five minutes in duration. After that I spliced and joined the spools to make a movie about twenty to thirty minutes long. It was a treat for all of us to congregate and watch movies on a sheet pinned to the wall. The stockmen were amazed to see themselves on screen. Jack Brand, the head stockman, gave me two turtle shells that he'd got from the Kimberley, in appreciation. I still have the turtle shells and footage which I had transferred to DVD by Duplication Station in Brisbane. I also had the voice tapes converted to digital format. It's very moving to look back on those years and listen to Mum and Dad's voices as well as Zak and Warren's.

Our fortnightly mailman was greeted with much excitement and anticipation. On board was the food order, but the highlight was the delivery of letters and tapes from home and the comics I ordered for the boys (*Donald Duck*, and *Betty and Veronica*). It was our connection with the outside world and we thought life was good. Because of the large stretch of dirt road before reaching the highway, the mailman was unable to reach us when it rained as the road became impassable. It was my job to do the ordering and keep sufficient supplies to last a month.

1981

As Grant was growing up I felt the need to have another baby to complete the family and for him to have some company similar in age. There were no young children at the station homestead. I was fortunate to fall pregnant again and on 20 March 1981 at 5.00 am I started having contractions. On the roll call at 7.00 am I advised the RFDS that my baby was ready to join the world and would they please come and collect me. By 9.00 am we were winging our way towards Carnarvon. At 5.30 pm Dr Board delivered Adrian Patrick weighing 6 lb 10 oz.

Like his brothers he was a beautiful baby boy and, as I knew he would be my last, he was very special. He was christened at two months of age in St George's Parish Church, Carnarvon. Yvonne and Tom Pullinger together with Zak were his Sponsors. He was *the Magic Pudding* in *the Adventures of Bunyip Bluegum* by Norman Lindsay! I nick-named him Puddy, because he had a round face, much like

I did as a baby, but he wasn't fat. Zak's nickname was Zakky. Warren was Mischief, because when at Limestone Cottage in Dandaragan, I once left him in the kitchen in his baby walker whilst I hung the washing outside, and he proceeded to turn our rainwater tank tap on, flooding the kitchen! Fortunately, the tank wasn't emptied. Grant was nicknamed Granticus. The boys still refer to each other as Zakky, Chiffy, Granticus and Puds or Puddy.

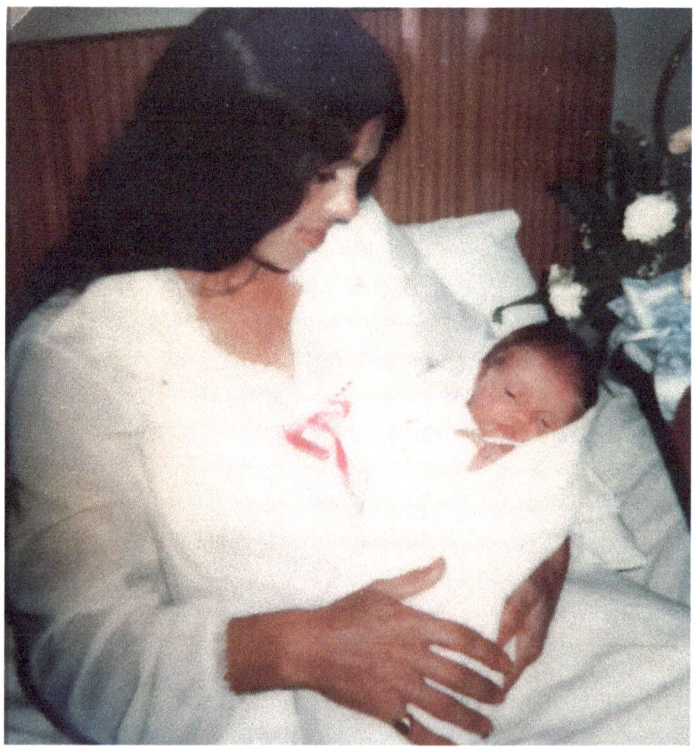

Elizabeth and Adrian in hospital

Elizabeth and Adrian (age seven months)

Adrian (age two weeks)

Warren and Adrian

Adrian

As with the other births, Ian was not present. My absence gave him the opportunity to drink freely. My friends, the Kearney family, went to advise him of the birth. They found him 'under the weather' and stayed with him until he sobered sufficiently to drive in to visit me and our newborn. It was then I realised that I couldn't continue ignoring the situation. I thought that with each new baby he would somehow come to his senses. I knew that he loved me deep down but couldn't control his drinking—he was an alcoholic. He needed professional help, so in our holidays I arranged for him to attend a rehabilitation course run by the Salvation Army. They conducted a lot of medical tests and asked me if I was aware that Ian had been drinking methylated spirits. I was shocked but finally understood how Ian appeared to be under the influence but hadn't touched the bottles of beer we had in the house. He used to start the thirty-two volt lighting plant at 5.30 in the morning. I found the metho hidden in the lighting plant shed. The course was conducted on a farm in the south-west of Western Australia and had the best recovery rate for alcoholics at the time. Unfortunately, Ian didn't stay the course and discharged himself halfway through.

Chapter 7
1981 continued

In 1981, at twelve years of age, and after six years of correspondence/School of the Air, Zak went to St Patrick's College in Geraldton as a boarder. It broke my heart to say goodbye. Warren followed suit two years later. After having spent all our waking hours together—eating, teaching, riding etc, I felt an emptiness. My two oldest sons had virtually flown the coop.

I loved Ian deeply but I couldn't carry on with the mental anguish that comes with living with an alcoholic—the moods, having to be constantly alert, watching for the excuse to have a drink. So began the exercise of concentrating on Ian's bad habits only, dismissing my feelings of love and his good points. It was a daunting task because he was the love of my life and the father of my children. But I knew that until he acknowledged his drinking problem, life would become intolerable and I had the responsibility of caring for and nurturing my children. It took six months of constant mental discipline, but I faced up to my dislike of Ian's behaviour and managed to dislike him in the end.

Warren, Grant, Elizabeth and Adrian (left to right)

Zak

Warren and Zak

1983

In April 1983 I flew back to Jersey to clear my head. I decided to complete my pilot licence and qualified as a private pilot in May. Grant and Adrian stayed at La Ferme (my sister Anne's farm) whilst I completed my lessons.

Grant, Adrian, Thomas, Jo Ann, friend (left to right)

My parents suggested that I return home to Jersey with the boys and start a new life. However, the lure of Australia had won me over and besides, the boys were Australian. Dorothea Mackellar puts it so succinctly:

The love of field and coppice,
Of green and shaded lanes.
Of ordered woods and gardens

Is running in your veins,
Strong love of grey-blue distance
Brown streams and soft dim skies
I know but cannot share it,
My love is otherwise.
I love a sunburnt country,
A land of sweeping plains,
Of ragged mountain ranges,
Of droughts and flooding rains.
I love her far horizons,
I love her jewel-sea,
Her beauty and her terror -
The wide brown land for me!

Ian and I decided to separate. Ian took the position of manager of Innouendy Station and I stayed at Wandagee. The stations were just over 500 kilometres apart by road. Each property had a pedal radio, and on weekdays roll call would be taken—the station occupants would reply to the Royal Flying Doctor Service base in Carnarvon to ensure all was well. Ian would answer the roll call before me as the stations were called in alphabetical order. After a couple of months he begged me to return to him and I arranged to meet him in Carnarvon with the young children. I couldn't believe it when I arrived and couldn't find him. I finally located him in a pub, drunk. That was the last straw as I had threatened to leave three times before only for Ian to promise it wouldn't happen again. I had wanted so much to believe him and took him back each time. He'd cut out drinking for a week or two but he wasn't ready for complete abstinence and so the cycle went on.

I returned to Wandagee and Ian returned to Innouendy. By then his drinking had taken over his life and he was asked to leave. I understand he was caretaker for a small coastal property up north for a while, but that too didn't last long. He went on the dole and began a relationship with an Aboriginal woman in Broome.

Chapter 8
1983

I was grateful to Joe Elliott, who owned Wandagee, for allowing the little boys and me to stay on until we decided what the future held. He and Mrs Elliott lived in Geraldton but Joe regularly flew around his properties, Wandagee on the Minilya River, and Mt Stuart and Kooline on the Ashburton River. He offered me the position of housekeeper at Mt Stuart, which I gladly took. However, I wasn't happy there and wondered how I could leave. Joe (twenty-five years my senior) was becoming controlling and possessive. I'm sure he thought he could buy me as, unbeknown to me at the time, he purchased Duck Creek Station (adjoining Mt Stuart) in my name. Understandably, all hell broke loose with his family over the purchase.

Around this time, Joe flew down to Geraldton and left Lloyd, the overseer, in charge. The Aboriginal stockmen and Penny (who moved from Wandagee) somehow got hold of a lot of grog and went on a rampage. Penny had also got hold of a gun and was going to shoot me. Terrified, I locked the homestead and hid under a bed, shielding Grant and Adrian, fearing the worst.

Lloyd was unable to control them but somehow, during a lull in the drunken attack, he managed to get the boys and me out. We hid under a tarpaulin in the back of his ute and hightailed out of there under the cover of darkness. As soon as we were away from Mt Stuart, Grant recalls lying on a mattress in the back of the ute for mile upon mile, watching the stars. We drove down to Wandagee. I was never going to return to the Ashburton.

Radio reception at Wandagee was spasmodic, at best, but one day I heard an advertisement for trainee broadcasters for women in regional areas, to be applied for at the Geraldton ABC Radio Station. I thought to myself, *Come hell or highwater, I'm going to get that job.* Joe had an empty cottage on his property outside Geraldton and offered it to me, complete with the largest carpet snake I've ever seen. There was a substantial rise in the carpet from one side of the loungeroom to the other. I started beating it with a broom to flatten the carpet only to find that it moved! Fortunately, it took off after its beating.

Regrettably, I was able to sell the ponies but had to leave poor old Sabre behind. The new overseer kindly took care of him. Sabre was crippled with arthritis and had to be put down six months later. He had been such a wonderful companion—it felt like losing a member of the family. The sale of the ponies was sad too because it meant the end of a chapter in our lives. Grant and Adrian were not destined to become bush kids and I was sorry about that. With Zak and Warren at school in Geraldton we were going to become city dwellers. It was nice though to enjoy 240 volt electricity, lighting whenever it was required and an abundance of good water for showering, but I did miss the bush.

After arriving in Geraldton, I immediately registered for the dole. I didn't have a job and needed an income. I felt ashamed as I stood in the queue waiting to register. But the dole did tide me over for the immediate future. I wrote to my parents and told them Ian and I had parted and that I would be seeking a divorce. We divorced in

May 1984. Ian came down to Geraldton and we finalised a maintenance agreement on May 28th. It was agreed that we should have joint guardianship of the children and I should have sole custody. A maintenance agreement at the rate of 120 dollars per week, apportioned equally between the four children, was also agreed to. However, I knew there would not be any money forthcoming as Ian was on the dole. We had been married for sixteen years.

In the meantime, I applied for the trainee position as broadcaster at the ABC. It took a few weeks to learn that I was one of two successful applicants. I was over the moon! I desperately wanted to be independent and leave the cottage at Joe's farm. That was when he told me he had bought Duck Creek in my name. I was stunned and silently fumed. I found out who his solicitor was, made an appointment, and told him that this transaction had been done without my knowledge or consent and that I wanted my name taken off the pastoral lease. I paid for the privilege!

Now that I was earning I decided that we needed a home of our own and so contracted to buy Unit 5, Shearwater, Tarcoola, a Cape Cod style townhouse on top of the hill, where the sound of waves could be heard. It felt so luxurious.

Zak and Warren were attending St Patrick's College and Grant started school at St Francis Xavier. I enrolled Adrian into Geraldton's family day care.

Warren, Adrian, Grant and Zak (left to right)

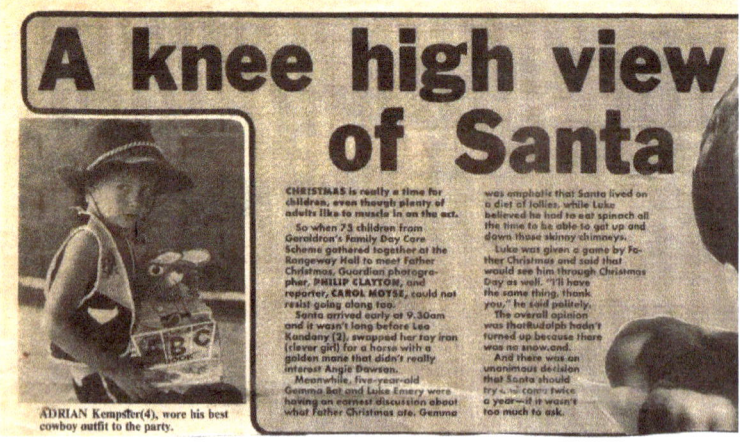

Geraldton Newspaper clipping, 1985

I enjoyed my training at the ABC but found it difficult to express myself at first, having limited adult conversations whilst on the stations. By the end of the training programme the ABC wanted evidence that the programme had been successful. They funded me to fly to the Mt Magnet and Meekatharra area and interview women who lived on isolated station properties. I was so grateful to be able to utilise my private pilot's licence. It was also right up my alley as I could understand and sympathise with ladies who were living under similar conditions and circumstances as I had myself. All interviews were enlightening but I particularly recall the honesty and depth of feeling spoken by Margaret Lacey, who was then the president of the Isolated Children and Parents Association in WA. The interviews were recorded and sent to ABC Radio Sydney where they were broadcast on the 'Outback and Outspoken' programme. The following is the introduction I prepared:

> I left Geraldton, Western Australia, on a beautiful clear sunny Monday at the controls of a Cessna 172, destination Mt Magnet, a gold mining and pastoral town, 350 kilometres east of Geraldton. The bumpy trip was due to thermal activity, an indication of summer around the corner. A prevailing easterly

headwind made the trip take longer than the anticipated 2 hours but at last I spotted Mt Magnet in the distance. I buzzed the town (circling at low altitude) to attract the attention of the fuel agent who immediately loaded a forty four gallon drum of avgas on to his utility and drove out to the airstrip 10 kilometres south of the township. He gave me a lift into Mt Magnet where I was then collected by Val Jensen and we drove out to her property, Wogarno Station, 50 kilometres to the south, where I stayed overnight and interviewed several ladies who were kind enough to drive over from neighbouring stations. The following morning I loaded the aircraft and set off over the top of Hill 50 Gold Mine. Three quarters of an hour later I approached Lake Austin, the large elongated salt lake which had water in it, most unusual, so I knew I was on track. I continued north over the vastness of the country, which has few distinctive land marks. The instructions on how to find Polele Station were, 'when I came across a large claypan, turn right and continue east until a shearing shed came into view, then Polele would be 5 miles further inland'. *Hooray*, I thought with excitement and relief as I spotted the homestead. I completed a low flying inspection of the bush strip just to make sure there were no potholes or kangaroos ready to jump out from a disturbed siesta. I landed, one and a half hours total flying time from Mt Magnet. The countryside looked magnificent with purple mulla mulla, vivid red Sturt peas with their black eyes in profusion, wattles in full blossom, carpets of everlastings and parakelia—the likes of which I have never seen before. The red, dusty earth was clothed in a magnificent array to celebrate the long years of nakedness.

Geraldton Newspaper, June 1984

Geraldton Newspaper, September 1984

After the completion of the training programme, I was offered a position in advertising and news reading by Noel Hardy, the advertising manager of GTW 11, the local TV station. I was very excited as I would help in producing commercials and put my broadcasting skills to good use.

I was enjoying my freedom and started ballroom dancing classes one evening per week. Joe turned up one night and called me out. I stepped outside to be confronted by a very angry man. He had found out about my visit to his solicitor and was trying to drag me to his car. I yelled at him to leave me alone, which made him more angry. Fortunately, a passing young couple could hear and see my distress. The young man got hold of Joe and told him to leave me alone or else he would call the police, whereupon Joe jumped in his car and took off. I was so grateful to that young man.

Chapter 9
Late 1985

One of the advertisers at GTW11 was Bed Post and the local franchise owner told me the franchisors were going to open a chain of stores in Queensland and that I could have one for one dollar to help establish the chain. I thought this would give me the opportunity to start afresh, away from Ian and Joe. Ian and I still corresponded and I encouraged the boys to write regularly but I knew he would not admit he was an alcoholic. He was happy that we kept in touch.

I wrote to my mother and she arranged the funds for flights and start-up money for a Bed Post store in Ipswich, Queensland. I put the townhouse on the market, packed up the furniture and made plans for the move. I told Ian I was moving to Queensland,

and Joe that I was returning home to Jersey. The furniture must be the best travelled as it has seen most of Australia from the inside of trucks.

Geraldton Newspaper, March 1986

We had acquired a beautiful, intelligent Siamese cat, Sam, who used to protect the townhouse from all and sundry. It was so amusing to watch him stalking a large canine who one day dared to enter the garden. Sam jumped on his back and clawed his private parts with his back legs. The dog took off howling and from then on would wander up the street, crossing to the other side when getting close to the garden and waiting until he was well past before crossing back again. I was unable to bring Sam with us but found a really good home for him. We were all upset to leave him behind.

As Zak was in his final year at school and had been asked to try out for the West Australian hockey team, I left him as a boarder to finish his schooling at St Patrick's. He would join us later.

Chapter 10
1986-1994

We flew the red eye special across the country from Perth, over Alice Springs, to Sydney. We stayed with a friend for a couple of nights and then headed up to Brisbane, where we rented a house in Karalee, overlooking the Bremer River. I enrolled the boys into St Edmund's College for Warren and St Mary's Primary School for Grant and Adrian. The boys were able to catch the school bus, which enabled me to set up shop in Brisbane Street, Ipswich.

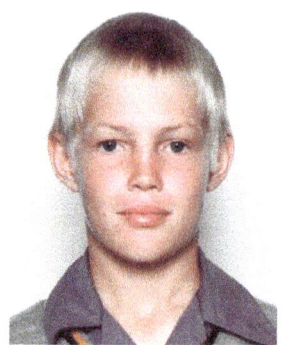
Warren

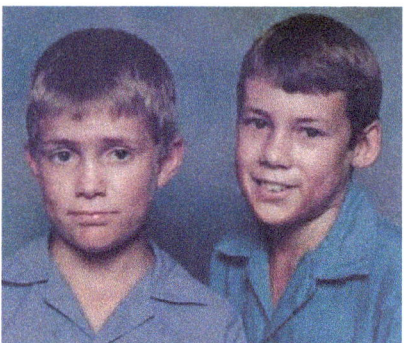
Adrian, Grant

Our furniture finally arrived and it felt good to have something constant in our lives again. I began unpacking and the boys took the packing material to the incinerator at the back of the house. When the incinerator was full, Warren went to the garage and got a jerry can of fuel, as he'd watched his father pour diesel on camp fires when starting a bush barbecue. Unfortunately, the jerry can contained petrol, not diesel. There was a huge explosion with terrible consequences. Warren had superficial burns to his hands, Adrian had burns on his right leg from the knee down and Grant suffered eighty per cent burns with fifty per cent of those third degree. His synthetic T-shirt had melted. I immediately put him under the shower, running tepid water. His skin peeled off like potato peelings. I called the Ipswich ambulance but having no immediate response I bundled them all into the car and drove to the hospital, frantically taking a wrong turn. It felt like an eternity before he was seen. Finally, he was covered in what appeared to be Alfoil and taken to the Mater Children's Hospital in Brisbane. We followed the ambulance in the car, praying for all I was worth.

Warren's hands were dressed, Adrian's leg was dressed and he was hospitalised. Grant was put in the intensive care unit where he was placed in a coma for three weeks. Seeing my children suffer and being at a total loss to help was the most indescribable pain I have endured. Warren and Adrian I knew would recover but Grant's burns were so severe that for the first couple of months the risk of infection was a constant threat.

After three weeks, once he'd regained consciousness, he was put into a single room because of a *Staphylococcus* outbreak. He was only eight years of age and just so brave. He was attended to by the most wonderful nurse, Claire. I was so grateful to her. Words can't describe the emotional ups and downs of not knowing whether or not my child was going to pull through.

My wonderful mother came to the rescue as soon as she could. She was able to look after Warren and Adrian. I phoned Zak and asked him to please come over to Queensland. He left school without fulfilling his ambitions and took over the role of father figure to his youngest brothers. He did a great job.

I stayed in the hospital at first then travelled back and forth from Ipswich. I had to employ staff to run the business, which wasn't ideal. A start-up business needs the owner to put in the extra yards to establish a client base. However, we muddled along for a few months. I didn't give a damn about the business. I just wanted Grant to survive.

Grant was in hospital for nine months, going to theatre twice weekly. The surgeons, Dr Lanigan and Dr Milne, would shave a little skin from his bottom (unburnt skin) and patch him up. Contractions were a huge problem especially under his arms, neck, elbows and knees, and had to be cut and released for many years to come. When Grant emerged from the coma, the first movie that engaged him was *The Never Ending Story*. I was so relieved to see him take an interest. He also avidly watched basketball on TV. The Brisbane Bullets visited his bedside and arranged for him to be picked up and transported to their live games at

Boondall. He was given court-side tickets and treated like royalty. This gave him so much to look forward to and a relief from the pain of his surgical procedures. His favourite player was Danny Morseu.

Grant and Danny Morseu

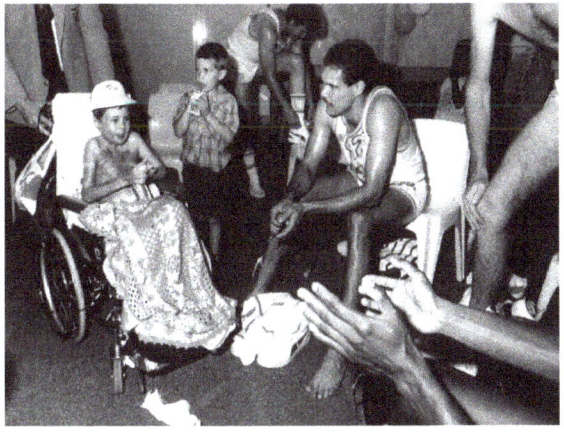

Grant and Adrian in Brisbane Bullets' dressing room

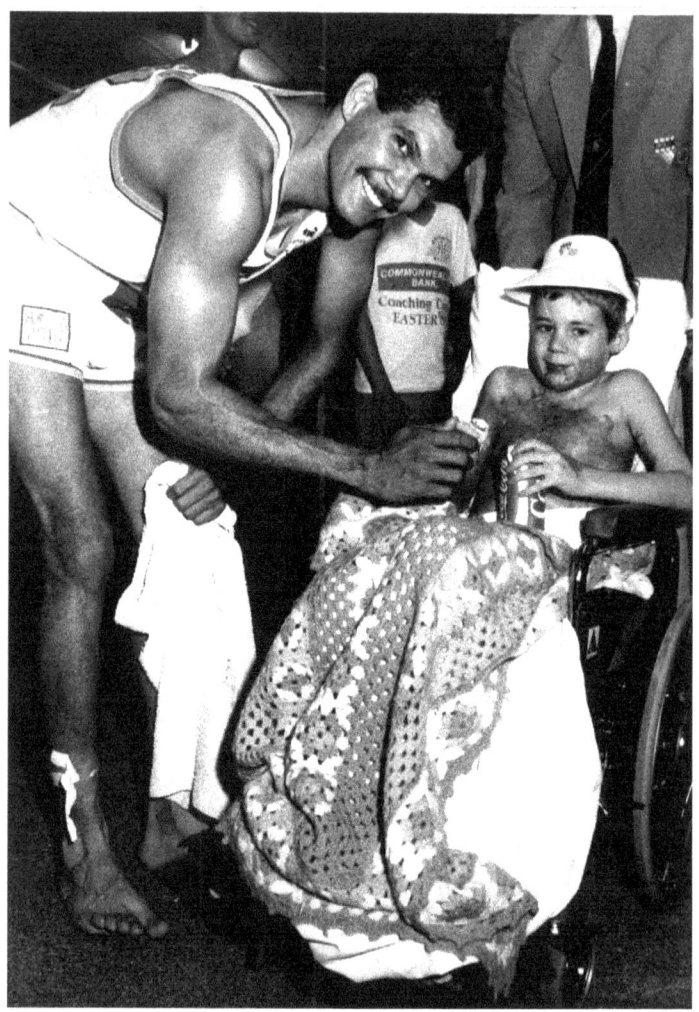

Danny Morseu and Grant

Chapter 10 1986–1994

Ipswich Newspaper, 1986

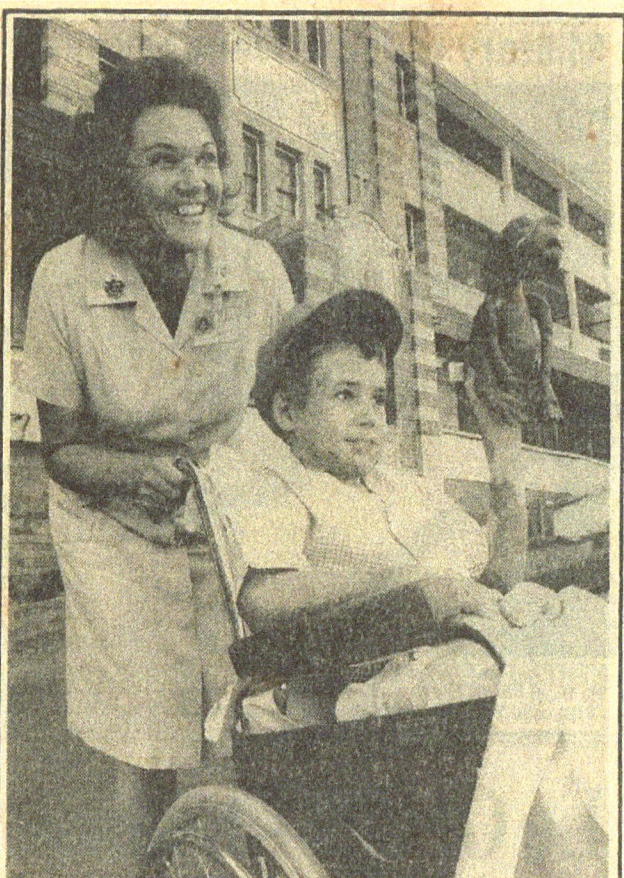

SISTER Claire Lees, of Manly, is happy for Grant Kempster, 8, of Karalee, as he leaves the Mater Children's Hospital after five months' treatment.

Look out Skeeter, here he comes

GRANT Kempster was discharged from hospital yesterday and more than anything else, was looking forward to playing with his dog Skeeter II.

Grant had spent four months alone in the infectious diseases ward at the Mater Children's Hospital. Before that he was in the surgical ward for a month.

Skeeter II was a gift for Grant's eighth birthday on July 15. He said his parents had taken the Jack Russell terrier to visit him in hospital.

On April 26, Grant received serious burns to 60 percent of his body after an accident near a barbecue. The accident was only a week after his family moved from Western Australia to Karalee, Ipswich.

The charge nurse of the infectious diseases ward, Kay James, said that since the accident, Grant had been to the operating theatre 50 times for intensive skin grafts and redressing.

Grant said it was great to be going home because he "didn't like anything" about his stay in hospital. But he did make a lot of friends, whom he would miss, he said.

Ipswich Newspaper, 1986

Mum had returned to Jersey and I returned to Bed Post in Ipswich during the day and drove to the Mater Hospital in Brisbane at night to see Grant who, thank God, was on the road to recovery.

Many factors contributed to my making the decision to declare myself bankrupt. Having to pay two full-time staff during my absence, together with paying for $30 000 worth of stock became a nightmare, literally. Zak helped me as delivery driver and installer (waterbeds were popular) whilst I operated the shop. Joyce Australia were supportive as they put their Pipeline range of children's furniture on consignment. I felt I was getting on top of things, when the $4611 tax bill came in. It was as though it was never going to end, so on 24 April 1991 I petitioned for bankruptcy. In the meantime the Bed Post franchisors had found a buyer for the business and all invoices were paid apart from the taxation bill. On reflection I should have approached the Taxation Department and requested a payment plan, which I have since learned is possible, but at the time I was tired and weary of the financial burden and saw bankruptcy as the only solution. I handed my passport in to the Official Receiver which meant I was bound by the bankruptcy rules for two years. I was discharged from bankruptcy on 21 July 1993. I felt human again.

Grant was now convalescing at home in his little Joyce foldabed until he was able to attend St Mary's Primary School with Adrian. Warren was attending St Edmund's College, Ipswich. The Principal, Brother Reardon, was a true Christian, kind and compassionate. He took Warren under his wing and visited Grant when he was at the Mater.

Grant was going to need more operations to release the contractures, which were a constant problem. He handled all this like a mature adult and went to the operating theatre willingly. I decided to move to Brisbane to be closer to medical facilities. I enrolled Grant and Adrian in St Peter and Paul's, Bulimba, and rented a house in Henderson Street, within cycling distance of school.

Joyce Australia offered me a position as Sales Consultant to the Woolstores in New Farm. I was happy to accept as the hours were ten until four and I could catch the ferry to go to work, which was delightful. The main advantage was to be at home for Grant and Adrian before and after school. Zak was working in sales for Bristol Paints and Warren had gone jackarooing at Minnie Downs, Tambo. You can take the boy out of the bush, but you can't take the bush out of the boy! One weekend we went down to Cunungra in Queensland to watch a rodeo and Adrian, aged six years, came fifth in the calf riding, which was great, particularly as he'd never ridden a horse let alone a calf.

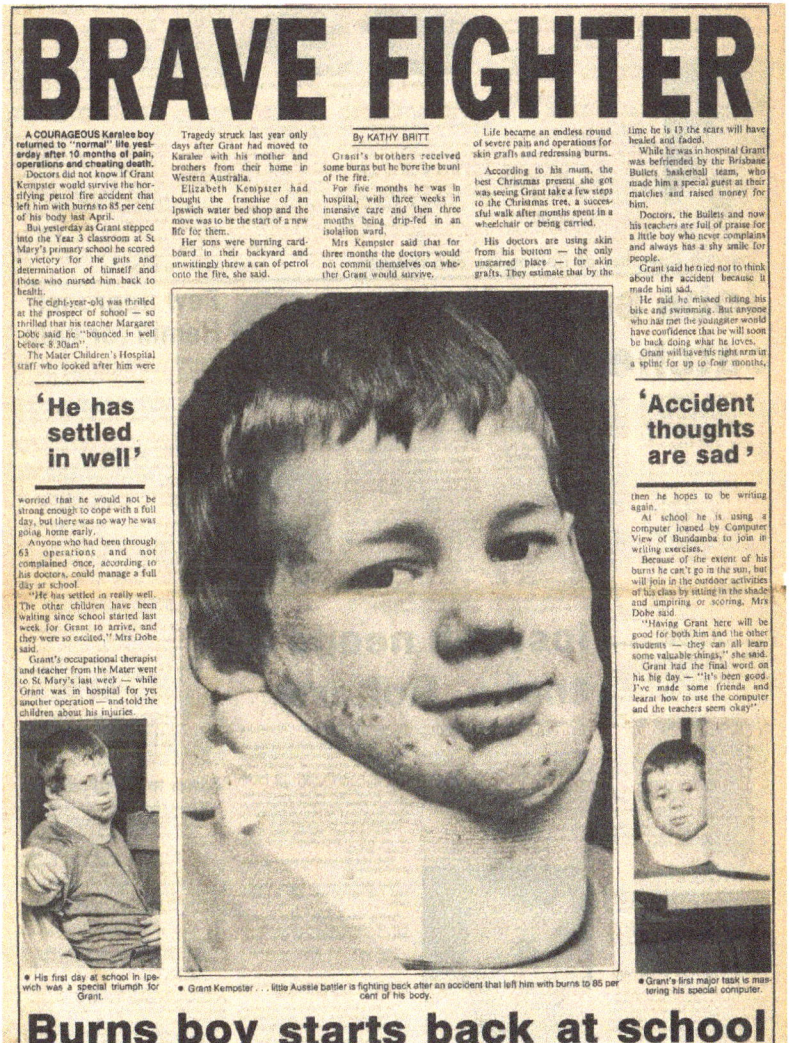

Ipswich Newspaper, February 1987

Ipswich Newspaper, 1987

We had been corresponding with Ian, who said that he would save for a plane ticket to come over from Broome. I was hopeful that perhaps he now realised the importance of family and responded that we would be delighted to see him, but that there were strict rules to be adhered to. He assured me he was 'off the grog' and that I need not worry. I prepared the spare room for him and anxiously awaited his arrival. He duly arrived and it was good to see him, although he had aged and had no front teeth. At first, all went well but after a couple of weeks I noticed a change in him. When I returned from work one day I was sure he'd been drinking and found that he'd replaced the alcohol in my canisters on the French dresser with tea. He hadn't changed. I couldn't cope with him and told him that he had to go back to WA, whereupon he told me that he had bought a one way ticket and had no money. So, I had to purchase a ticket for him to return to Broome, which he reluctantly accepted. I reassured him that we would still correspond but that there was no chance of a reunion.

Adrian calf riding

I had been looking at property for sale as I saw paying rent as dead money. Zak was agreeable to help and so on 5 February 1992, he purchased 59 Beauvardia St, Cannon Hill. In reality we were joint owners but because my bankruptcy was still in effect it had to be in his name only. We paid $118 500 for the property, which was terribly run down. Over time everything was replaced including the roof, but we could call it our own.

Chapter 10 1986–1994

59 Beauvardia Street, Cannon Hill, QLD

Zak had become engaged to Kylie Ann Cornish and they wanted to live together so he needed to be released from the mortgage.

On 30 June 1994 we had the property valued at $128 000. After costs we had $4000 equity each, so the property was transferred into my name and Zak was kind enough to allow me to repay by instalments from my wages.

To help make ends meet I registered as a homestay with a number of international language colleges in Brisbane. On the whole it was a rewarding experience, meeting students from Europe and Asia, helping them assimilate and learn the language. Grant made friends with Ramiro, a lovely Spanish young man and I still keep in touch with Elisabeth from Northern Italy and Maeko from Japan. In fact, Maeko made Beauvardia St her Australian home, visiting three times in three years.

Zak and Kylie

Chapter 11
1986-1994 continued

In order to keep my pilot's licence current, I joined the Darling Downs Aero Club in Toowoomba and passed the flight review on 17 August 1986. However, I couldn't afford the time or money to keep up flying until September 1987 when I joined the Queensland Aviation Club (QAC) at Archerfield. I enjoyed taking part in the competitions held at Kagaru in a Cessna 152 hired from Flight Training Australia. Robbie Robinson, president of the Qld Aviation Club, wanted a formation team, so, after instruction, on 23 January 1988 I was endorsed for formation flying by Chief Instructor Humphrey Maltman from Flight Training Australia. There were four of us in the formation team and I was Robbie's wingman. We took part in the FM 104 radio station's Sky Show together with a fly past over Fort Lytton, which was very exciting.

Flying had become my passion and release, in particular formation flying, which took a great deal of concentration and precision. On 15 September 1990 we conducted a fly past for the marriage of QAC members Ian and June. This was in preparation for a display formation of fourteen light aircraft on 23 September 1990 over the Brisbane River, to commemorate the Battle of Britain. We were the smallest bunch and at the tail-end after all the magnificent warbirds, which created such turbulence that it took all my wits and strength to fly straight and level. What a buzz!

I became so enthused that I considered becoming a commercial pilot—quite impractical being over forty years of age and a sole parent. However, I did attend the commercial theory classes at Archerfield and passed the very difficult test, comprising meteorology, aerodynamics, navigation, air legislation, etc. These were all foreign subjects as I had not done science at school.

By this time Robbie, who was an air traffic controller at Archerfield, and I had become firm friends. He suggested we enter the Sunshine State

Air Race held over two days in August 1991. We hired a Cessna 172 from Flight Training Australia and entered—Robbie as navigator, Terry Maguire (another enthusiast and friend) as spotter and myself as pilot. Rather than a race it was more like a treasure hunt, where approximately thirty light aircraft took off at intervals from Cherrabah Resort, near Warwick, in search of the answers to a quiz, before returning to Cherrabah. We overnighted at Cherrabah and set off the next day in our quest to find answers to another set of questions. For example, 'At lat ---- and long ---- there's a homestead with what colour roof and how many sheep in the yards?' Our final destination was the Maroochydore Aero Club. The winner was the team with the most accurate timing (you had to work out how long it should take to reach each turning point before leaving and submit your flight plan to the organisers) and the most accurate answers to the quiz. It was so much fun, although quite nerve racking at times. At least we didn't get lost!

*Plaque and photo to commemorate the
1989 Sunshine State Air Race*

Apart from Grant needing regular operations, life was looking rosy. In 1987 Zak, at eighteen years of age, wanted to spread his wings and went to Jersey on a working holiday. He stayed at my sister Anne's farm, and it was some initiation I believe. He worked at Elizabeth Castle as an assistant gardener. There was an incident where, one evening when following his cousins on the windy country roads, he crashed his motorbike. Fortunately, he was unscathed but the motorbike was a write-off.

Joyce Australia, based in Perth, held a competition for the best sales figures and I was gob-smacked to find I'd won a trip for two to Hawaii. I decided to take Warren with me in September 1989. We hired a car, with Warren as chauffeur, and had a great time although he was disappointed he wasn't allowed into the bars or nightclubs, being just under eighteen years of age. The legal drinking age is twenty-one years in the US. Seeing Pearl Harbor was very moving but the highlight for me was doing a bicycle ride from the summit of Haleakala Crater (the largest dormant volcano on earth) above the clouds, round and around and around down through the mist to ground level. We watched a lava flow turning into black sand on impact with the sea, two months after its eruption. It was a wonderful ten days. I thought Maui was magical.

Warren on top of Haleakala Crater, Maui

Everything was coasting along nicely when the Woolstore management decided they didn't need consultants, but preferred to employ their own staff. Fortunately, they put me on the payroll. Because the Woolstore had a huge range of furniture and bedding, a lot of it imported, they advertised heavily and therefore needed an advertising agent. I befriended Maaike Vromans, who I consider a close friend still today. Robbie and I were wanting to enter another Sunshine State Air Race, so I approached Maaike to ask whether any sponsorship could be forthcoming. She immediately jumped on board and wanted to be part of the team. She approached 4KQ Brisbane radio and Wonderest bedding manufacturer who were kind enough to support us. Maaike was our Spotter.

Top: Robbie and Maaike   Bottom: Maaike and Elizabeth

We entered three annual Sunshine State Air Races and had an absolutely marvellous time. Before the final dinner and presentation, held on the last night, there was a fancy-dress competition. Thanks to Maaike's artistic bent, we were a source of great amusement to the crowd, as Maaike made up a skit for us to play out. It was so much fun. The act that really sticks in my mind was so simple but so clever.

We wore black caps embroidered with 'Guide Dog' for Robbie the navigator, 'Spot' for Maaike as spotter and 'Top Dog' for me as pilot. All skits were brilliant, with simple tools as props. For example, the motel curtain rod was used for Robbie's white blind cane and some powder mixed with foundation for our white doggie muzzles. Maaike should have been a stage director!

Top: Top: Elizabeth, Robbie and Maaike

Bottom: Elizabeth, Robbie, Maaike (left to right, far left of picture) and other pilot competitors

In the meantime, Warren decided he wanted to attend Gatton Agricultural College and was accepted in 1991. He met his future wife, Samantha Rose Hughes, while attending the college.

Elizabeth, Sam and Warren (left to right) at Lake Mackenzie, Fraser Island

Both Grant and Adrian were now attending Iona College. Grant formed the Nomads Cricket Team, which comprised my four boys, schoolmates and Robbie as wicket keeper. They continued to play warehouse cricket at Tingalpa for years and were highly successful. I loved taking lunch on a Sunday and watching my boys demonstrate team spirit and generally barracking for the Nomads. Kylie, Zak's fiancée, was the team scorer and great at the job. In fact, whenever there was a dispute over the score, the Warehouse umpires always backed her figures.

Top: The Nomads Cricket Team
Bottom: Zak, Robbie, Adrian, Grant and Warren

Life was very busy, but I had time to renovate the house, removing plasterboard and asbestos to reveal lovely tongue-and-groove walls, which I painted. The old linoleum revealed beautiful pine flooring, which I had polished. There were four bedrooms upstairs and I was able to get the house dug out downstairs, making for a huge entertainment area, two bedrooms and a bathroom, which Warren kindly installed for me. The boys happily settled into their bachelor pad and their mates regarded Beauvardia Street as their second home.

Adrian in Iona colours

Grant in Iona colours

Chapter 12
1994-2001

My lifestyle was changing, becoming more hectic and demanding, or perhaps I was just getting older! Retail stores were now operating Thursday and Friday nights and opening on weekends. I felt family life was beginning to suffer. For instance, I had to forego watching the Nomads play cricket on many a weekend due to work commitments.

However, the highlight of 1994 was the marriages between Zak and Kylie and Warren and Samantha. Warren and Samantha tied the knot on September 17th, at St Stephen's Church in Ipswich. We were very blessed that Mum, my three sisters and their husbands and Yvonne, my second cousin from Perth, all came over to join in the celebration. My sister Anne sang *Ave Maria* for the couple. It was a wonderful occasion.

*Grant in year twelve,
aged seventeen, 1996*

*Adrian in year eleven,
aged sixteen, 1996*

Warren and Sam's wedding

Zak and Kylie married on December 17th at St Peter's Anglican Church, Wynnum, followed by a reception at the Manly Yacht Club. Mum was able to stay for the wedding, but the other members of the family had to return to Jersey and WA, understandably. It too was a wonderful occasion.

Zak and Kylie's wedding

After leaving school the two younger boys continued working at Pizza Hut, Cannon Hill, rising to supervisor status. Warren had had his initiation into adulthood when he went jackarooing, and Zak when he went to Jersey in 1987. In 1999 Grant went over to Jersey in search of a similar experience and he worked for my nephew Jimmy, packing Jersey new potatoes in the packing shed. It was hard graft, working fourteen-hour days and only eight hours on Sundays. He was the only non-Portuguese employee and got paid a pittance. Jimmy sat in the office watching the Ashes cricket whilst Grant hurriedly packed the twenty-kilogram bags, trying not to spill the potatoes as they came down the conveyor belt at a rapid rate. He spilled them on several occasions, causing the whole conveyor belt operation to cease, whilst everyone helped him pick up the fallen potatoes. After three months of back-breaking work it was time for standing of the seed potatoes for next season's crop. He feigned a back injury as the thought of standing up for twelve hours a day, not socialising with anyone, was too much.

On his second trip with Adrian in 2001 he crashed my mother's Mini (she had left it to the family), costing him two month's wages, which was more than the car was worth. During this trip Adrian found himself a job working at the Trinity Arms Hotel as a barman. He basically worked for free because most of his wages were spent behind the bar, although he did save enough to go on a Contiki tour across Europe. He enjoyed visiting the historical cultural sites and took many photographs. He, unlike his brothers, didn't crash a car or bike whilst in Jersey, but made up for it later in Australia, when in his first car, a red Gemini, Adrian and his mates found themselves in a precarious situation. This would become known as 'The Belmont Ditch Incident'. The car had careened into a ditch and they were discovered hanging upside down, held in by their seatbelts! Apparently, a cat had run in front of the car.

Another piece of information later came to light. While driving my little one tonne truck (Adrian did a stint as truck driver for me) he rolled it when going around a roundabout and somehow it miraculously righted itself. All of these incidents were shades of their mother in her youth.

My boys were growing up and establishing themselves. Grant was accepted into the Federal Police Force and relocated to Canberra, so just Adrian and I remained at Beauvardia Street. Robbie asked if he could board, as he had retired from air traffic control and I had a room to spare. Robbie and I had a good chat and we decided to start a small transport company, Rokem Transport, which we would both operate. My first truck was a little old one tonne Mazda, bought from the second-hand car yard around the corner for $1000. Stubbie, Warren's old dog, was my offsider. The business took a while to establish but we were successful in the end, having a good client base. We were eventually able to upgrade to new Isuzu four-tonners with extra-long trays. We specialised in carrying electrical equipment such as switchboards and reclosures. We also carried on flying, enjoying participating in competitions held at Kagaru.

Left: Robbie in Mazda
Right: Elizabeth and Stubbie in Mazda one-tonner (left to right)

Chapter 13
2001–2008

Life continued much the same for several years, working hard to keep the business expanding and looking after students.

After Dad had passed away in 1983, Mum came to spend winters with us, continuing to do so until into her ninety-third year, when she too passed away. We were having a barbecue in the garden to celebrate Kylie's birthday on 14 January 2001, when there was a phone call from my sister Anne. I was gutted. We all expected Mum to make her one hundredth birthday. It took a couple of years to stop continually thinking of her. I was so fortunate to have had such wonderful, caring parents.

Mum, in her ninetieth year, Grant, Zak, Warren, Adrian (left to right), Elizabeth

Headstone of Elizabeth's parents' grave

Various nephews and nieces from Jersey also came and stayed, so the Jersey connection continued. In 2007, Warren asked if I'd like to spend Christmas in Jersey with him, Samantha, and their children. It was a generous offer which I readily accepted. My immediate family had grown to encompass four grandchildren, Zak and Kylie's Harrison (2000) and Claire (2004), and Warren and Samantha's Thomas (2002) and Lillian (2004).

When we got off the plane in Jersey, we thought we had landed in the Antarctic as the crisp, cold air forced its way into our lungs—it was minus two degrees! However, it was a wonderful feeling to be back on the soil of my birth, and so good to see my nephew Robbie and niece Susan's smiling faces to greet us. We drove in convoy to La Ferme and on opening my sister Anne's kitchen door I was certain I was hallucinating as the first of many, many faces I saw were Zak, Kylie, Harrison and Claire, then my sisters Anne and Ruth, my nephew and Anne's son Johnny, and Derek who had been a long-term fixture on the farm and consequent close friend of the family. I was just trying to take in this huge surprise when, lo and behold, Adrian walked in through the door. I couldn't believe my eyes! I thought Grant should be here but knew he was on duty in Canberra, when I saw a figure strolling across the front lawn and I recognised that gait. To have my entire Aussie family in Jersey was beyond my wildest dreams. I was gob-smacked, speechless, overwhelmed and very, very grateful. Warren and Sam had treated the whole family and I had had no idea!

Christmas Eve

Christmas Eve day was spent in the woods where the stream trickled down into the large frozen dam. Robbie organised us with military precision. We all took turns with the clippers and ladders gathering an enormous sack of holly, ivy and butcher's broom laden with berries.

Samantha, Kylie, Harrison, Claire, Zak, Lillian and Thomas (left to right)

Top: Samantha gathering broom
Bottom: Robbie and Warren holding the ladder steady

After that all hands were on deck in the press house decorating it with the fruits of the forest and Christmas lights, turning it into Aladdin's cave. We spent the rest of the day preparing for the feast on Christmas Day. Jo Ann (Robbie's wife) put the enormous turkey in her Aga at Le Paysage at midnight and Anne cooked the roast pork and vegetables in her Aga at La Ferme. Johnny, who lives at Oak Shadows, brought some very new potatoes from one of his fields. We also had homegrown carrots, parsnips, broccoli and the boys' and my favourite, brussels sprouts, much to the chagrin of my daughters-in-law! At 6.30 pm we all went to St Martin's Church—our beautiful family church (built over 1000 years ago) where the Billot family celebrates its hatches, matches and dispatches. The short candle-lit service, coupled with familiar carols sung by everyone with gusto, resounded through the arches and Alan Mollet played the organ as well as he did when I attended in my youth.

Adrian and Grant—winners 'most berries broom'

Anne standing next to statue of St Martin

Christmas Day

Christmas Day was a great family reunion as Anne's huge family and ours feasted after descending on Jimmy and Susan's at Le Perchoir for champagne and nibbles. As Grant's godfather, Jimmy presented Grant with a mountain of presents as high as himself, all boxed-up containing thirty presents, for each of his thirty years! Johnny won first prize for devouring his piled plate back at La Ferme. Needless to say it took all afternoon to savour the feast, after which we played 'Starlight', 'Pass the Scissors', 'Animal Families' and mystery games until midnight when the boys went over to Le Paysage to watch the Boxing Day Test at the MCG—Australia versus India.

Victoria, Holly, Grant and Tom (left to right)

Boxing Day

The local Boxing Day test, held at the Farmers' Field between the Farmers and Australia, was a huge success and resulted in a draw. The Aussies batted first. Warren retired at fifty-two with a total score of five for 142 runs after twenty overs. Warren won man of the match with his superb batting. Kylie did her usual great job in keeping an accurate scorebook. The spectators enjoyed the spectacle whilst sipping mulled wine and eating Christmas cake in the club house. I walked back to La Ferme after the game was over, via Rozel Valley, along the beautiful steep winding narrow lane.

Top: The Boxing Day test teams, the Farmers versus Australia
Bottom: Warren, Grant, Kylie (scorer) and Harrison (left to right, in forefront)

Top: Warren, Samantha, Grant, Adrian, Zak, Kylie (back row, left to right); Thomas, Lillian, Elizabeth, Harrison, Claire (front row, left to right)

Grant and Adrian, my nephew Johnny and his children Zander and Tory turned up at 7.00 pm together with my nephew Jimmy, his wife Susan, and children Holly, James and Chuggy. Andrew Picot, another nephew, arrived with my sister Ruth who had already had a three-course meal. Nephew Robbie and his wife Jo Ann arrived with their children, Thomas and Ruth, and we all sat down to a buffet meal in the press house starting on the second turkey, gammon and a huge variety of salads. The second Christmas pudding was enjoyed together with sumptuous cheeses. Games such as 'Squeak Piggy Squeak' and 'Celebrity Head' were played well into the night, culminating with the boys being magnetically drawn into the sitting room to watch the cricket. Midnight was late enough for me to turn in!

December 27th

Another annual sporting event, this time soccer, was held: the Perchards versus the Richardsons. The Richardsons were long-time family friends and farming rivals. Zak, Warren, Grant and Adrian played for the Perchards, with Zak as the goalkeeper. It was a cracker of a game with Grant scoring the first goal for the Perchards followed by an equaliser from the Richardsons. Grant scored three goals—a hat-trick—which won the game for the Perchards. The cold, damp, fierce wind didn't deter either side from an excellent game, which was celebrated later round the cosy fires of the Royal Hotel where everyone enjoyed an enormous delicious dish of shepherd's pie and chips, compliments of the hotelier. Considering there were two full teams plus supporters, I thought it was a grand gesture.

Perchards (yellow): James, Zak, Johnny, Adrian and Philosh (left to right)

Robbie suggested a walk around Queen's Valley (the town water supply) which Sam, Kylie, myself and the four grandchildren were eager to participate in. It was a wonderful walk around the dam filled with ducks, moorhens and a solitary cormorant who claimed the little rowing boat moored in the middle.

December 28th

Grant and Adrian, who were staying with Johnny at Oak Shadows, arrived in a borrowed VW and we drove three cars via La Chasse and Waverley to Gorey for a family outing. We spent the day at Mt

Orgeuil Castle where the 'little' ones dressed up in medieval clothing and charged into the castle on foot, winding their way through tunnels and many, many steep granite staircases. The stalactites drip-dripped their continuous flow through the ceilings of the dungeons. We eventually made our way to the top after listening and watching films on the building and development of the 800 year old castle. Sir Walter Raleigh was Governor of Jersey during Queen Elizabeth the First's reign and was eventually hung, drawn and quartered after some twelve years of his original sentence by the Queen, who had been green with envy over his falling in love with one of her maids-in-waiting who bore him a child. Such fascinating history. The 360 degree view from the top of the towering castle is magnificent, enabling detection, in fine weather, of invading French ships leaving the French coast.

We had lunch at the Dolphin Hotel (the moules mariniére were delicious) and afterwards drove into St Helier to change some money and buy medication for the flu, which the family was succumbing to.

Top: Princesses Lillian and Claire passing Knight Grant
Bottom: Warren making Sir Wuller Ruleigh's acquaintance

Mont Orgeuil Castle

December 30th

Thomas Perchard had given me a beautiful birch as my Chris Cringle gift and we had a tree planting ceremony at the Farmers' Cricket Ground, attended by most of the family. It was one of many trees being planted around the cricket ground, which my nephew Jimmy established.

In the afternoon we drove down to St Catherine's Chapel where we left the cars and walked through St Catherine's Woods, belonging to Rozel Manor, down the bridle path to St Catherine's Bay, where Grant and Adrian skimmed pebbles across the water. I used to swim my pony there and also learnt to water ski in my teens—fond memories.

Planting Birch tree in the Farmers' Cricket Grounds

We then walked around the coastline to St Catherine's Breakwater—a huge, long pier built by the English in Napoleonic times, together with Martello towers, to keep the French out. It was a beautiful peaceful scene, altogether different from the night Bernard and John Larbalestier lost their lives in tempestuous seas whilst trying to escape during the German occupation of Jersey during the Second World War. We continued around the coastline, cutting across to the top of Rozel Valley and onwards past La Ville Bree, where my sisters and I were brought up, down the bumpy lane and back to La Ferme.

Top: Tom, Grant and Jimmy (left to right)
Bottom: Sam, Lillian, Adrian and Grant (left to right) at St Catherine's Bay

December 31st

We went to Les Avenues, my sister Ruth's home, and saw the progress being made in the total renovation of her house. The inside had been gutted and modernised but the outside granite façade remained the same. We walked down the steep and winding track, following the coastline to Egypt, which is an extremely rugged and beautiful area of land, and ended at La Fontaine Tavern where we lunched. I enjoyed my favourite, moules mariniére. The building is absolutely gorgeous—one of the oldest taverns in Jersey. Dark, cosy rooms warmed by huge open fires are linked in rabbit warren fashion by tiny doorways, which we had to stoop to enter. I'm certain it would have been a popular venue for pirates.

We spent the afternoon preparing for the evening's festivities at La Ferme, which began with Anne's sloe gin (I'm very partial to it), followed by beer and wine to wash down the delicious curry which Johnny had made. Both he and Zak had the flu, poor boys. Nevertheless, a crowd of approximately forty people enjoyed the curry followed by delicious sweets and cheeses.

What a night was spent in the press house! We sang *Auld Lang Syne* and played 'Apple bobbing', 'Cork bobbing', 'Nail hammering' and many other old-fashioned games of yesteryear. It was a wonderful evening and brought back memories of the Christmas fetes at St Martin's Parish Hall.

Top: Egypt
Bottom: Family trek at Egypt

Top: Warren, Sam, Kylie and Zak (left to right)
Bottom: Claire, Harrison, Lillian & Thomas (left to right)

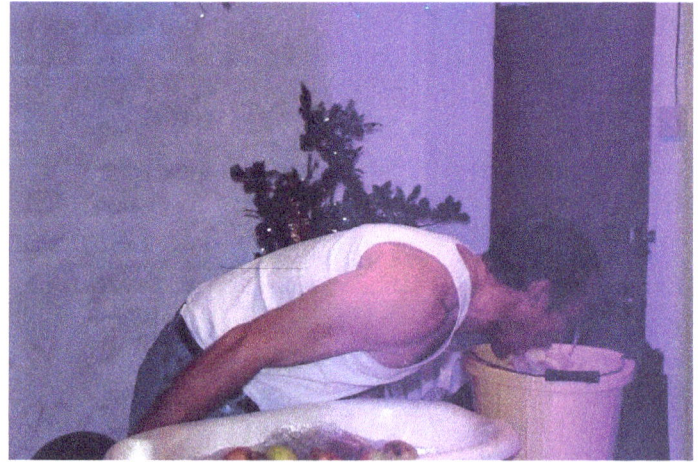

Top: Anne cork bobbing
Bottom: Warren apple bobbing

New Year's Day 2008

The first of January began well for us but was worrying for others. Hezron, the Jersey-sponsored

Kenyan doctor, was sheltering with other Lua tribal families in his house and trying to stay alive amid the massacre—turmoil and chaos I can't imagine.

We went to Jimmy and Susan's for lunch for another roast turkey accompanied by roast potato, sweet potato, parsnip, peas, carrots, cauliflower cheese, brussels sprouts, leek and butter beans, herb stuffing, chestnut stuffing, devils on horseback, pigs in blankets accompanied by cranberry sauce, all washed down with superb French wines. This sumptuous banquet was followed by Christmas pudding and Christmas chocolate log. I had to waddle back to La Ferme to try and work off my total indulgence.

On our return to La Ferme, Anne and I sat down and prepared seven enormous chancre crabs and six huge spider crabs for a fruit de mer. Robbie and Jo Ann brought seaweed as a base for the platters, which were then decorated with the crabs, giant oysters, mussels, prawns and whelks on a seabed of ice and lemon wedges. Another feast was enjoyed by twenty-seven family members. I couldn't do it justice as my stomach was groaning over this eat-athon.

Top: Jimmy lighting the Christmas pudding at the family table, 2007

Bottom: Jimmy, Holly, Chuggy, Marion, Derek, Zak (left to right)

Top: James devouring crab claw
Bottom: Susan with the good stuff

After dinner, the games began once again. Grant and Adrian, followed by Sam and Kylie, played 'The Naughty Schoolboy/Schoolgirl'—hilarious. They had everyone in fits of laughter. 'Ibble Dibble' was then played but I piked out at midnight, not being able to hack the pace anymore. The last of the players were still active around 3.00 am. Come morning there were many bodies stretched out on all available sofas throughout the house and press house.

Too much for Jimmy!

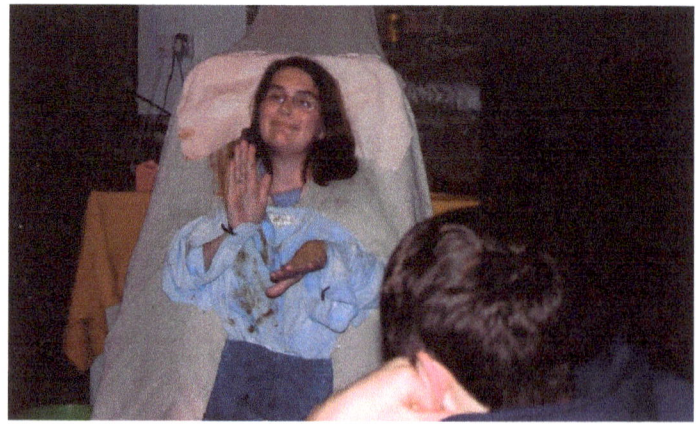

Top: 'Naughty little schoolgirls' Kylie and Samantha

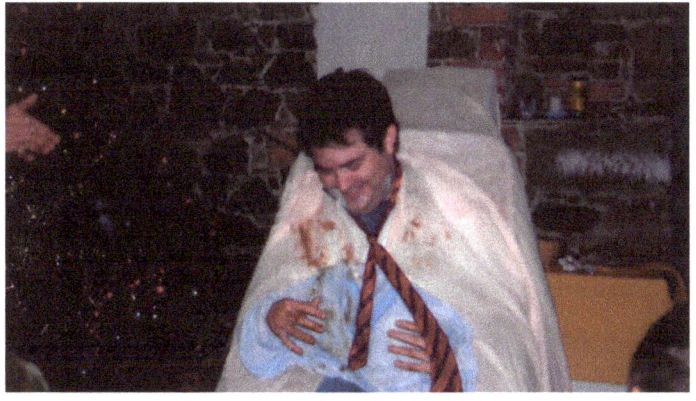

Bottom: 'Naughty little schoolboys' Adrian and Grant

January 2nd

Sam, Kylie and I went into St Helier to take advantage of the sales and to arrange the booking for our French trip, leaving Monday, returning Friday. I wanted to show the family a small part of France, in particular Mont Saint Michel in Normandy, a World Heritage listed monastery.

Anne generously treated the whole family to the pantomime *Dick Whittington*, bringing back real memories of my youth when I used to sing and dance with Madeleine Le Riche's troupe as part of the children's cast for the annual panto. The panto was a great success with all the children shouting 'look behind you' when the evil king rat (brilliantly portrayed) was stalking Fairy-Nuff who suddenly appeared every time Sarah Sloppit or Watt uttered the words 'fair enough'. It was an excellent production. The costumes and dancing were superb, spiced up with the odd political comment.

Unfortunately, most of the family spent the rest of the night barking and coughing—the flu had caught up with us. So we had to be well-medicated for our trip to France. I missed out on Senator James Perchard's (Jimmy, my nephew) guided tour of the States of Jersey and the chambers, instead getting prednisolone and erythromycin from the doctor.

January 3rd

I spent the morning organising our trip, due to leave on January 7th. Because it was off season I was able to secure an extremely good package at Hotel l'Abbaye in Plancoet—four nights B & B accommodation, based on two family rooms and a triple room.

Anne and I dined with the Seigneur of Samarés Manor and other members of the Slow Food Club. This is where people take turns in hosting a dinner. It was a lovely evening meeting up with old school friends and getting home at midnight.

January 6th Plough Sunday

We all went to St Martin's Church for Plough Sunday. Robbie and Jimmy carried in the plough to be blessed and to pray for a good season. We enjoyed mulled wine with the parishioners after the service, then a quick visit to the Royal Hotel across the road before heading back to La Ferme for a roast pork feast followed by mince pie or bramley apple jelly pie smothered in cream, custard or ice-cream. Our waistlines were increasing daily! We sat in the sitting room by the fire playing board games, reading or watching the TV after dinner.

January 7th

We awoke to terrible weather which resulted in a postponement of our trip to St Malo by Condor ferry, from 7.00 am to 7.00 pm. Even so, it was extremely rough and the poor grandchildren were seasick. We overnighted in St Malo, collected our hire cars, a seven-seater Citroën People Mover and a four-seater Toyota, and drove to Hotel l'Abbaye, Plancoét, a converted nunnery.

Hotel l'Abbaye

January 9th

After a delicious continental breakfast we headed off to Mont St Michel. It really is a spectacular sight, even when first sighted from a long distance. We all enjoyed exploring it, starting from the base and meandering through the many halls and chapels until we arrived at the sanctuary near the top. We heard chanting behind closed doors and took the liberty of peeping through the keyhole whereupon a sea of white-robed monks could be seen singing in unison with the purest of boys' voices, making for sounds and visions of many times past.

Top: Mont St Michel

Bottom: Samantha, Warren, Kylie, Adrian, Zak, Claire, Grant (left to right); In front: Thomas and Lillian; at Mont St Michel

Top: Lillian, Adrian, Kylie, Grant at Mont St Michel water fountain
Bottom: Grant at Mont St Michel entrance (souvenir alley)

January 10th

Dinan Day. It was market day in this beautiful old city which I'd once travelled to on a school camp. The biggest juicy black cherries still make my mouth water. After giving the children a bit of freedom on the swings and roundabout in the park, which resulted in poor Lillian vomiting, we enjoyed a delightful meal in a lovely little café on the riverbank. Grant was so enthralled with his dish of raw beef that the chef gave him a second helping free of charge.

Top: Adrian, Grant, Harrison and Claire (left to right)
Bottom: Elizabeth, Harrison, Claire, Lillian, Thomas (left to right)

January 11th

It was back to St Malo for our return to Jersey, but due to inclement weather the trip was postponed to the following day. We were pleased to catch the Condor ferry the next morning, but as soon as we left port the seas began to swell and it wasn't long into the journey before the majority of passengers succumbed to seasickness, claiming all the sick bags and toilets. We were relieved to berth in St Helier and retrieve our land legs, although Warren in particular remained a shade of green until the next day. Robbie had organised a pheasant shoot for Zak and Warren that afternoon, so off they went.

A few days later it was time to return home to Australia. We had experienced the most memorable moments thanks to my Jersey family who embraced us all with open arms and gave us such a wonderful time.

Top: Zak with pheasant and Warren.
Bottom: La Ferme

Chapter 14
2009

Grant was now working for the Federal Police based in Canberra, although he completed a couple of deployments to the Solomon Islands. He was able to obtain and pay for the official Jersey flag which was used during the Commonwealth Games held in Melbourne in 2006. It was a wonderful surprise when he arrived home with this flag, which took pride of place on my sitting room wall.

He wanted to take me back to Jersey again, this time via France. From Heathrow we caught the channel crossing train at Victoria Station and marvelled at the fifty-kilometre underground underwater crossing. We stayed in Montmartre at the Tournee du Chat Noir. I loved feeling French. There were steep, narrow cobbled streets connecting the white domed Basilica of the Sacre-Coeur to its artistic flock below. We visited Le Lido, a cabaret and burlesque show where my second cousin Darna Pallot had performed for a number of years. I don't know how they can keep up the pace as it's such a strenuous show, but it was well worth the visit. We dined like professional foodies, loving French cuisine. However, Grant's choice of Andouille de Guemere looked, smelled and tasted like pig's bottom. Grant didn't flinch and polished it off. Meanwhile I thoroughly enjoyed escargots, my favourite entrée. We stayed in a chateau near Amboise, having a great time exploring the wineries and taking a balloon ride over the area overlooking deer bounding through the forest, gliding over our chateau and taking in the town of Amboise. It seems you can't turn a corner in the Loire Valley without coming across a magnificent chateau, all so different, opulent yet enchanting. We drove back to St Malo and caught the ferry, taking a boot load of Amboise wine to share with our Jersey relatives. It was a wonderful trip and we had such fun.

The official Jersey flag used at the Melbourne Commonwealth Games, 2006

Grant enjoying Andouille de Guemére

Escargots—yummy!

Vintage bottles in Caves Duhard, Amboise

Getting ready for lift-off

Chateau des Arpentis where we stayed—small and intimate compared to some of the chateaux of the Loire

Chateau des Arpentis

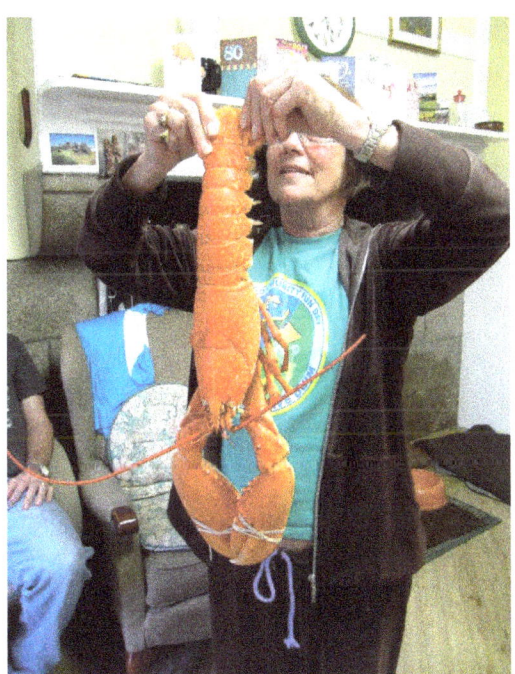

*Enormous birthday lobster caught by Philosh,
Elizabeth's grand nephew*

Chapter 15
2012

We returned to Jersey as a family for my sister Anne's eightieth birthday celebration. It was a grand occasion held in a marquee in the front field of La Ferme. Anne was regarded as the head of the family now and was loved and admired by all who knew her well. It came as no surprise that she was awarded an MBE by the Queen for her dedication and influence, as head of the World Jersey Cattle Bureau, in promoting the Jersey cow.

We enjoyed family barbecues, being the height of summer. Philosh, the family fisherman and my grand-nephew, provided seafood for such occasions. He presented me with a lobster for my birthday which would have measured two feet in length. I had never seen such huge crustaceans.

Johnny put on a hog roast at Oak Shadows, and Brodie decorated their whole house with Australian paraphernalia, e.g. sign posts pointing to Sydney, Brisbane, Melbourne and Perth. It was a delightful and fun setting.

Oak Shadows—Aussie style

Hog roast

R.J.A. & H.S.

A magazine page capturing Anne meeting the Queen

Anne's eightieth with Elizabeth's family

After the celebration we flew to London, did a little sightseeing then drove to Powys, Wales to visit my niece and goddaughter, Marjorie Morris and her husband Phil. We stayed in Norton Manor, a Jacobean house dated 1854, which felt very grand, although somewhat spooky according to the grandchildren. Overlooking the grounds, across the meadows, reminded me of Thomas Gainsborough's painting of sheep lying down, dotted underneath an enormous ancient tree, probably oak. It was a beautiful, peaceful setting. He certainly could have set up his easel and created a work of art there. We spent a lovely evening with Marjorie and Phil and then set off the following morning for the Lakes

District. We had to detour due to constant heavy rain and consequent flooding, making the roads due north impassable. I felt sorry for the farmers and their poor livestock, many of whom were lost in the flooding.

We eventually got to the Lakes District, which was shrouded in cloud, and stayed in Keswick. We visited Hill Top, the home of Beatrix Potter and the Saddleback Slate Quarry and museum at Threlkeld. We took the mine tour and rode on the miniature steam train. It was a marvellous excursion. Zak and Kylie bought slate number plates for their letter box in Australia.

Back row: Grant, Adrian, Zak, Kylie, Elizabeth, Warren, Samantha; Front row: Thomas, Harrison, Lillian, Claire

We left the Lakes District and continued up the west coast of Scotland to Cairnryan where we caught the Stena Superfast Ferry to Belfast, which took just over a couple of hours. We had acquired a passenger—a 'Gruffalo' toy, who was our mascot.

Adrian and Gruffalo

We hired a couple of cars and drove to Buncrana, where Robbie and Jo Ann had built a holiday house. Jo Ann, having been born and brought up in Northern Ireland, was equally at home in Ireland and Jersey. They met us in their lovely home where the shenanigans continued. We must have brought good weather with us as family barbecues and outings were not marred by inclement weather.

Visiting the Doagh Famine Village was a stark reminder of how harsh times were for families in the 1840s. We walked the path along Lough Swilly where huge oysters (seemingly on steroids) had been gathered for oysters Kilpatrick. We also visited the Grianan of Aileach, a stone fort sitting on top of a hill, giving panoramic 360 degree views. It dates back to 1700 BC, before the Celts, and is believed to be a burial monument.

Map of north-west Ireland showing Buncrana where Robbie and Jo Ann have their holiday home

The boys had their obligatory game of golf at the Ballyliffin Golf Club, Ireland's most northerly golf course, which boasts two championship links courses and an excellent nine hole par three course.

After our wonderful stay with Robbie and Jo Ann, who had always found room for us at Le Paysage on our Jersey visits, we headed off to Dublin.

Robbie and Jo Ann's house

Gruffalo. Jo Ann, Robbie, Jenny (back), Thomas and Ruth (front)

Fresh oysters—compliments of Rudiger, the German husband of one of Jo Ann's sisters who is a great chef and provided us all with beautiful meals

Robbie, Jo Ann, Samantha, Harrison at the Guinness factory

Dublin is such a lovely city, full of history and charm. We visited the Guinness factory, a mind-boggling establishment. Unfortunately, both Warren and Grant were sick and so not able to enjoy the experience.

We flew back to Jersey the following day, after a hectic but wonderful trip, and then prepared for our long flight home. Thomas and Lillian suffered from travel sickness which made their journey particularly arduous.

On our last day and night in Jersey we had a seafood day. We went to La Rocque looking for oysters and winkles. Cousin Phil brought over some lobsters and crabs that he caught at work and we all had another HUGE feast!

Kylie, Jo Ann, Adrian, Zak, Samantha, Robbie (back row); Claire, Harrison, Lillian (front row)

Lobsters, crabs and winkles

Chapter 16
2012 continued

I was back in time for the Ekka (the Royal Queensland Show), Queensland's largest and most loved annual event, attracting on average 400,000 people. I used to love taking Mum there on her annual visit and watching her re-judge the Jerseys! The steer being ridden around in the grand parade was such a beautiful quiet beast, I imagine he was hand-reared. The grand parade was a marvellous display of hundreds of different species parading around the huge ring, after they'd been judged. I loved the wood chopping too. Those men displayed such skill and came from all over the country and overseas to compete.

There were so many events and displays that one would have needed ten days to appreciate everything.

The Children's Corner contained all sorts of friendly furry animals, including pink 'chooks' who had their feathers dyed especially for the occasion and proudly strutted themselves around, showing off. Lillian and Thomas loved the Ekka too. However, the public holiday 'People's Day' had to suffice as it was back to work the next day.

I enjoyed being a truck driver, carrying precious loads to their destination and being off-loaded by, on the whole, friendly people. As my partner Robbie had passed away in December 2010, I had reduced the client base and only carried for Schneider Electric and NHP who, although large companies, were happy with the service I gave, encompassing the Brisbane metropolitan area, the Sunshine Coast and the Gold Coast. It is good to recall, when I'm passing those areas, delivering to places such as the Port of Brisbane, the Mater Children's Hospital, Energex depots and relatively new shopping centres, where reclosures and switchboards provided essential electrical services. I had my grandchildren as offsiders whenever possible and used to tell them, when crossing the Gateway Bridge, to look out for the Troll because he would be trip-trapping over the bridge at any time! Although they were little, I'm not sure they believed me.

Jersey cows at the Royal Queensland Show, Brisbane

What a load of bull! Royal Queensland Show, 2012

The woodchopping event, Royal Queensland Show, 2012

Trotting racing, Royal Queensland Show, 2012

Chapter 17
2013

My dear sister Anne had not been at all well after receiving chemotherapy treatment a couple of years previously. I am so grateful to Robbie, her eldest son, for contacting me by Skype at the end of March, a few days before she passed on. I didn't know what to say but felt close to her as she lay peacefully on her bed. Her immediate family escorted the hearse, on foot, from La Ferme through the property to her beloved St Martin's Church where she was laid to rest—a journey of approximately three miles.

I was able to attend her Memorial Service in July when the remainder of her ashes were spread over the top field overlooking the farm and the coast of France beyond. She would have been proud of her sons and daughter for this celebration of her life. She is not forgotten.

Elizabeth and Anne, 2012

Whilst there, we attended the wedding of Thomas (the son of my nephew Robbie and Jo Ann, and my sister Anne's grandson) to Claire in Trinity Church, on July 20th. The sun shone on the couple and it was a glorious summer day. The reception was held in a huge marquee on the front lawn of La Ferme. Warren and Samantha, Grant and Adrian all attended. Adrian flew over from Australia just for the weekend, as he couldn't take more time off from his job as a Human Resources Advisor.

My sister Ruth and I decided to go on a cruise up the Douro River on the Viking Hemingway from Oporto all the way to the Spanish border. We flew to Lisbon, Portugal and coached up the coast via

Coimbra to Oporto. We were entertained over lunch by the professors of music from Coimbra University, which I believe is one of the oldest universities in Europe, if not *the* oldest. They played Fado, summed up by the word 'saudade' in Portuguese, which translates into a feeling of longing, melancholy or nostalgia—very deep and romantic. I love the music which is played by classical guitar, bass guitar and Portuguese guitar accompanied by a soulful soloist.

Portuguese architecture is very attractive and very Moorish, sparkling white in the sun with contrasting red roofs. The churches exhibit Baroque styling—so ornate and powerful.

We continued to Oporto, my favourite city, where we sampled port in the famous Sandeman outlet, before boarding the Hemingway.

University of Coimbra, Portugal

University of Coimbra, Portugal

I had never been on a cruise before and found the experience to be beyond my expectations. We travelled on a small craft which docked in many interesting places along the Douro River, travelling at night so we could experience many and varied excursions during the day. There were no children on board. We made a lot of friends but I found that Teresa Chalecki from New Zealand and I had a great deal in common. In fact, we were the only Antipodeans on board. The Americans in Michael Reagan's party (yes, Ronald Reagan's son) were great fun and we danced on board until the wee hours of the morning. The crew was fantastic.

Sandeman Port Outlet, Oporto

Judy (American friend), Teresa and Ruth

We disembarked at Regua for a tour to Vila Real, site of the famous Mateus Palace, as depicted on the Mateus Rose wine bottles. This stunning palace was the home of the last Count of Real. We docked at Barca d'Alva near the Spanish border after travelling through spectacular countryside with sheer rock formations on both sides of the river. The beauty and history of the terraced vineyards, originally cut into the hillsides by the Romans and still worked by hand because of the steepness, was awe inspiring.

Cooking class—famous Portuguese custard tarts

The Mateus Palace

Terraced vineyards—Douro River, Portugal

We took a full day excursion by coach to Salamanca, the beautiful Spanish city which sparkled like gold in the sunshine from afar. We visited the Old and New Cathedral (both built from the 1500s to the 1700s) and listened to beautiful haunting choral music. Historically, Salamanca goes back to the Middle Ages, but is a cosmopolitan and multicultural city with a large population of international students. We also visited the market, which was so interesting. There was a lot of saucisson on display—I had previously thought it was a French specialty. On our way back to Oporto we disembarked and visited Lamego, a small town known for its baroque Sanctuary of Our Lady of Remedies, dating back to the fourteenth century and still used by pilgrims today.

Lamego, Portugal

It was such a fabulous ten day tour/cruise that I would recommend it to anyone. Portugal is still relatively untouched and people are pleased to interact and show visitors their beautiful country. Ruth flew back to Jersey and I flew back to Australia and back to the reality of working for a living!

I had written to Ian to advise him of Anne's passing. Warren had been corresponding regularly and Ian told him that he had had to give up the grog because he had throat cancer and that he was on medication and in remission. Warren kindly offered to pay for his airfare to Brisbane together with accommodation for as long as he wished, which Ian gladly accepted. We met on several occasions and although I felt sorry for him I had no feeling of love left. Sam and Warren were very good to him and he loved the attention from Thomas and Lillian. He'd missed out on his beautiful children, let alone grandchildren, all these years. He stayed for a couple of months but wanted to return to Broome, which had now become his permanent home.

Grant, Adrian, Ian, Zak and Warren (left to right) at Roma Street Parkland, Brisbane in 2012

Harry, Thomas, Lillian and Claire, 2012

Chapter 18
2013 continued

I had kept in touch with Maaike even though I was no longer employed by the Woolstore. A party of her friends had booked the Solway Lass tall ship, to sail the Whitsundays and Maaike suggested I might like to join in. They brought their own chef, so we dined like kings. Barbecued wagyu beef and a bag of fresh oysters kept in a sack in the sea and eaten when required, were just a taste of the delicacies we enjoyed, washed down with bloody Marys. We were twenty-one people in total. The only description suitable was that this was an adventure in paradise. As it was now August it was whale watching season. One of the guests took the photo below of a magnificent whale which breached close to the ship. It was 'designer' weather. The bluest of blue sky merged into the horizon so that it was nearly impossible to tell where the sky began and the sea ended. We went snorkelling, an experience I'd not had before, and it was just magical. The coral mothered shoals of little iridescent fish and we were ignored by most, except the majestic giant Maori Wrasse 'Elvis', who was a favourite among divers in the Whitsundays. He appeared to be almost six feet long and allowed me to stroke him and take a photograph with my underwater camera. I was thrilled.

We had left Airlie Beach and sailed passed Hook Island on to Blue Pearl Bay where we snorkelled. We rounded Hayman Island and continued south passing Lindeman Island to Shaw Island. We hooked up our sails, which was no mean feat, and sailed to Hamilton Island where we docked and replenished our water, emptied cisterns and did all the necessary restocking, including more tomato juice and vodka for bloody Marys! We then sailed to South Molle Island and did a very long bush walk to the lookout, which displayed the Whitsundays in all their glory. There was an Aboriginal midden with paintings and Errol Flynn had written his name and date in the rock, just after the war. We berthed at Nara Inlet and overnighted in the beautiful peaceful calm waters. One could have been on a mill pond. The next day a number of the men and Maaike, took on a Tarzan and Jane role and literally jumped ship! They used a long rope and swung off the deck with whoops and gesticulations before launching themselves into the deep sea down below.

Map of the Whitsunday Islands

At night we entertained ourselves. There was a dress-up box of pirate paraphernalia. We had such fun. I chose to be Jack Sparrow from the Pirates of the Caribbean and challenged Captain Hook (Maaike) to a duel for the hand of Maid Marcia.

The Solway Lass

The Whitsundays

Setting sail

Top: Andrew taking a leap of faith
Bottom: Overnighting Nara Inlet

Humpback whale breaching

Top: Maori Wrasse
Bottom: Elizabeth and friends snorkelling

Elizabeth (Jack Sparrow) and Maaike (Captain Hook)

Maaike

Chapter 18 2013 continued

Elizabeth and Marcia

I still communicate with Marcia by playing Words with Friends on a daily basis. We're able to keep in touch even though we're worlds apart. She lives in the US and I live in Australia. The Whitsunday trip was magical and blew all my cares away. It is truly paradise.

Chapter 19
2014

Maaike had organised a trip to New Zealand in February for the annual Art Deco Festival in Napier, Hawkes Bay, where tens of thousands of people revel in the 1930s atmosphere. The whole city embraces the event and everyone dresses accordingly. She warned me that I needed to prepare and pack an Art Deco wardrobe before leaving Brisbane. Fortunately, Susan and Jimmy Perchard (my nephew) were visiting us before my departure and Susan designed, selected and made the accessories. She's very artistic and talented.

We flew from Brisbane to Auckland, hired a car and drove 450 kilometres along the most picturesque scenery to Napier through Hamilton and Rotorua. Before reaching Rotorua we visited

Hobbiton, a fictional village, which appeared in JR Tolkien's *The Lord of the Rings* and *The Hobbit*. The set was built for the films on a farm near the little town of Matamata. It's very realistic.

Top: Steve, Damonica, Elizabeth, Maaike, Andrew (left to right) at Hobbiton

Bottom: Riding among the mountains

We went horse riding among the Tongariro mountains. What spectacular scenery. I can understand why so many Jersey people emigrated to New Zealand, which is similar in topography to Jersey, but much magnified. There are a great many Jersey dairy farms too.

At Rotorua we had a splendid time. We went to the hot springs and immersed ourselves in the soothing, bubbling pools, washing off the mud packs we'd applied to our faces. I spent a whole afternoon in the Rotorua Museum, being fascinated with learning about Maori culture.

Andrew, Maaike, Steve, Damonica, Elizabeth (left to right) at Rotorua

Maaike and her partner Andrew had a time share house on the northern shore of Lake Rotorua, where we stayed. In the twin lakes of Rotorua and

Rotoiti fishing for brown and rainbow trout is highly regarded. Our next-door neighbour had been fishing and presented Maaike with a beautiful brown trout. The chef on the premises kindly smoked it for us overnight and one of our party, Steve, turned it into a risotto the next day so that the five of us could have a taste. I love smoked trout and, being fresh, it just tasted so good. On one of Maaike's previous visits to New Zealand she had befriended a man named Wally from the Redeemers Motorcycle Club (religious bikies) who had a boat. He took us across Lake Rotoiti and left us there for a couple of hours. We had a swim in the lake, a beautiful peaceful isolated spot, and bathed in the hot springs. He collected us again and we put ten dollars in the honesty box.

Maaike had another surprise in store for me. She'd booked Kaituna Cascades for a grade five white water rafting event. I had no idea what to expect but felt lucky to be alive afterwards! It really was a great experience, but not one that I'll be repeating anytime soon.

Smoked trout for supper—caught in canal at Rotorua—delicious

Chapter 19 2014

Here we go! White water rafting

Resurgence!

Hanging on for dear life!

Phew! We live for another day

We continued on to Napier, enjoying the scenery, following a beekeeper moving his hives and being followed by many vintage cars. It seemed everyone was going to Napier. We rented a house on the main street overlooking Hawke's Bay, where we were in the thick of the Art Deco festival. Napier is known as the Art Deco capital of the world. In 1931 an earthquake measuring 7.9 on the Richter scale flattened the town and many people lost their lives or were badly injured. The city was rebuilt in Art Deco style. At the festival there are outdoor concerts, vintage car parades, fashion parades, Great Gatsby picnics and so much more.

We registered for the bicycle ride along the foreshore. Maaike, sitting in the fish bike's basket with Andrew pedalling her along, stole the show.

Maaike and Andrew on fish bike, Elizabeth in red, Napier

Elizabeth and friend

I was gob-smacked at the number and variety of vintage cars on display. I believe they were driven from all over the North Island especially for the occasion. There is no word for the quality of restorations other than outstanding. Maaike and I would have loved to have driven off in a beautiful Rolls Royce!

Another highlight of our holiday was taking part in the Mission Wineries Harvest Festival. This was a great venue, featuring 'The Battle of Britain' concert. The concert comprised Billy Ocean, Leo Sayer, Mel (Spice Girls) on behalf of England, and Ronan Keating (Boyzone) and Sharon Corr (lead singer of the Corrs) from Ireland. We arrived in the late afternoon by tractor, organised by the winery to transport guests, and set up a picnic in the beautiful grounds. As darkness fell the stage lit up and Leo Sayer performed under the blanket of darkness illuminated by millions of sparkling stars. It was magical.

Maaike, Elizabeth and beautiful Rolls Royce

Maaike, Elizabeth, Andrew, Steve At Mission Wineries

Elizabeth, Maaike and Andrew

Elizabeth and Maaike at 'The Battle of Britain' concert

I loved New Zealand. Maaike and Andrew had put together a great itinerary—it was jam-packed with wonderful experiences that I'll never forget.

Upon returning home I received advice from the nursing home in Broome that Ian had passed away during my last few days in New Zealand. It was very sad news and I felt deep regret. Zak and Warren flew over to Broome to make the necessary arrangements.

Chapter 20
2014-2015

Adrian was working for a mining company as a 'fly in fly out' human resources advisor. He decided to buy a new townhouse in Cannon Hill in the East Village Development and moved in in October 2014. Grant, who had left the Federal Police Force, shared with him. I decided to sell the place on Beauvardia Street as it was far too big for me. Warren had renovated the front of the house, making it saleable. I made the decision to buy in Charters Towers so that I could see more of Zak, Kylie and the children, who were now living there. The idea was that I would commute for holidays between Brisbane and the Towers, a fourteen hour drive, so I would be able to spend more time with family, and I would continue Rokem Transport by employing a driver.

59 Beauvardia Street, Cannon Hill

Number 59 Beauvardia Street eventually sold on 12 February 2014 after much hassle and is now no longer there. The house was removed on the back of a truck and two Hampton style homes were built on the site.

I missed looking out of my kitchen window and seeing the family of frogmouths who had made my garden their home and who nested annually in my poinciana tree. I wonder what happened to them.

Tawny Frogmouth

I didn't think the house would take so long to sell, so I had purchased another Queenslander in Charters Towers in September 2014. Twenty-one Davies Street, Richmond Hill, Charters Towers was larger than I expected and needed a great deal of work, but the bones were good and I thought it would be nice for the family to stay, when they visited.

21 Davies Street, Richmond Hill, Charters Towers

I stayed with Zak and Kylie for a couple of months whilst renovating. Warren made the fourteen hour drive up from Pine Mountain with new ceiling boards for the kitchen on his roof rack. He totally renovated the kitchen and put a new shower in the bathroom. The property had to be rewired, then family and friends helped repaint internally. After having the floors sanded and polished, I was set to move in and organised my furniture to be brought up. I employed painting contractors to paint the outside and slowly landscaped the garden. I was settled and happy, but my business wasn't doing well so I closed it down and sold my remaining truck.

It was a strange feeling that I had virtually circumnavigated the country to return to near our original starting point, Cloncurry. Zak's first teaching position had been at Distance Education, Charters Towers, and Kylie is now HOD Arts at All Souls St Gabriel's School, Charters Towers.

Our world began to fall apart when Zak suffered his first stroke on 31 May 2014 and his fourth on 17 November 2014. He had suffered from Crohn's disease and had had thirty centimetres of bowel removed at thirty years of age. Although we went to Brisbane, an accurate diagnosis could not be made after the strokes. It took Dr Richard White, a neurologist in Townsville, to correctly diagnose Zak with cerebral vasculitis. Zak was immobile after his last stroke. He couldn't walk or talk. We were beside ourselves, especially Kylie, who took leave from work and sat by Zak's bedside for months. I looked after Harry and Claire and drove them into Townsville to see their parents each weekend (a three hour round trip). Zak recovered sufficiently to be released from hospital and is home again. He did suffer brain damage so is unable to work, but he is with us, thank God, and has made great strides in his recovery.

It was during this time that I thought pony riding might be of benefit to Harry and Claire. So, I bought Miva Helou (Lou), a 14.1 hand palomino

Arab gelding for myself and Richmond Brown Eyes (Richie), a brown quarter horse/stock horse, as he was less flighty, for the children. We joined pony club and enjoyed the rallies.

Claire on Richmond Brown Eyes

Claire, now a teenager, has grown out of horses and so I made the decision to sell Lou. He went to an excellent home in Townsville. I now ride Richie and entered the Charters Towers Show last year and was happily surprised to win some ribbons.

Miva Helou

To add to the menagerie I have an Oriental and a Siamese cat. Above: Harry and Makita

When selling Lou, I met a lady who had a litter of fox terriers for sale. I had had a foxy named Pepsi after Warren's old dog had passed away, who was my offsider in the truck in Brisbane. He was a great little guard dog—if anyone went near the truck he would make nasty, growling noises. No one would dare put their hand inside if I wasn't there. He had passed away at twelve years of age and I swore I'd never get another dog. However, my heart melted when I saw these gorgeous little pups and so I now am the proud owner of Soda! Soda accompanies me on rides with Richie in the bush near my house.

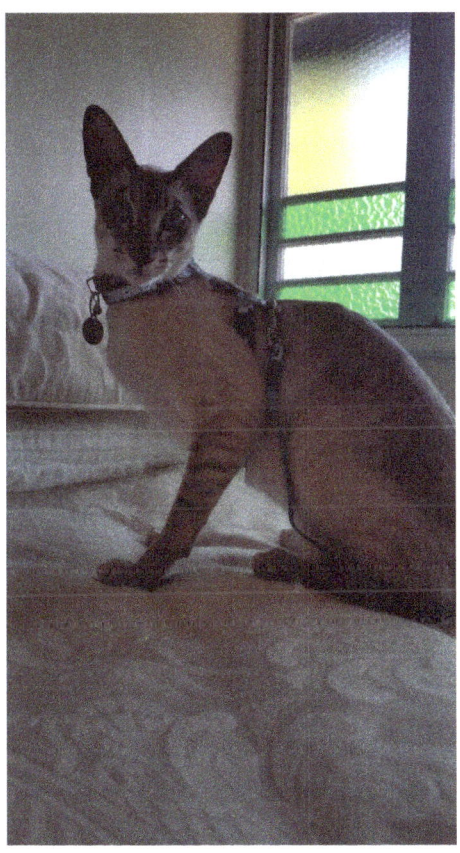

Simba

Elizabeth riding Richie

Soda and Ritchie

Chapter 21
2016-2020

When Adrian bought his townhouse, he was courting a lovely young lady, Chloe Parkinson. The relationship flourished and on 24 September 2016 they married in St John the Baptist Anglican Church, Bulimba. After the ceremony they walked down Oxford Street to the Bulimba Ferry where they were ceremoniously ferried across the Brisbane River to the reception at Gusto da Gianni's, Hamilton. The Council generously gave free passage to the wedding party. It was a beautiful wedding and had international representation. Robbie, Jo Ann and Ruth Perchard together with Phil Mourant came over from Jersey. Janet Ferguson from Canada and Jun Abe from Japan had been Rotary exchange students with

Chloe in Hungary in 2004 and also came over to join in the celebration.

Adrian and Chloe Kempster and the Kempster family

Assorted photos from Adrian and Chloe's wedding day

The Best Man's speech. Grant was quite the comedian, and brought the house down.

Grant regaling stories of a now lost bachelor life that he used to share with Adrian

On 30 March 2018 Patrick Adrian Kempster came into the world. He's now a very bright, bubbly two year old with tons of energy. We communicate with WhatsApp but it's not the same as seeing them in person. He's a joy to his parents and a delight to his grandmother.

Patrick Adrian Kempster

In the meantime, Grant had purchased an apartment in the same complex as Adrian and Chloe. They could wave to each other from their respective balconies. Grant had met and was engaged to lovely Leanne Read. They formalised their relationship at Iona College Chapel, where Grant had attended senior school. A family friend had offered his beautifully restored home, Whepstead Manor, for the reception. It's a grand old house renowned for its ghost sightings over the years, including that of a Chinese worker thought to have hanged himself as well as Mrs Burnett, the original owner's wife, whose presence has been felt along with her distinct lavender perfume. No ghosts spoiled the reception, which was a hoot! It was wonderful that my grand-niece (Robbie and Jo Ann's daughter) Ruth Perchard, being the Jersey connection, came over especially for the wedding.

Grant and Leanne's wedding day

Adrian, Grant and Michael singing from the rooftop!

Big Bird, alias Adam Taylor (Leanne's brother-in-law) appears

Elizabeth, Chloe, Leanne, Ruth, Claire, Lillian (left to right). What an effect!

Grant and his mates from Canberra

Adrian, Elizabeth, Grant, Warren and Zak, at Grant's wedding

It goes without saying that it was another joyous wedding, with the last of my four sons to commit themselves, each to a wonderful woman.

On 16 May 2020 Joni Anne Kempster made her entrance into the world. She's a beautiful baby and so good. I'm sure she's a little angel in disguise!

Chapter 21 2016–2020

Joni Anne

Elizabeth's two youngest grandchildren, Patrick and Joni, at Joni's Christening at St Oliver Plunkett Church, Cannon Hill, September 2020

Conclusion

Looking back on my life, it's certainly been an adventure I could not have predicted when growing up as a young girl on a dairy and potato farm in Jersey, Channel Islands. I do sometimes wonder if I had stayed in Jersey, how different my life would have been. I would have always followed Ian though; I was young and in love. I would never have imagined having to fight to hold on to my marriage and keep my family together. Coming from a safe and trusting background, where I was brought up to believe that love would cure all, it came as a harsh reality that this is not always the case. Although ultimately I had to let go of Ian, my boys fulfilled my need to love and be loved. Having had their respective hardships, I am proud to see my four sons all as successful men, husbands and fathers and am very grateful to have been blessed with healthy, happy grandchildren.

I am also blessed to enjoy good health and am very happily settled in Charters Towers with my horse, dog, two cats and large garden. It has brought me back to my roots and I appreciate the lifestyle that country life offers. I am particularly grateful to Susie, June, Jan, Karlene and Sherry for sharing true friendship with me. We have wonderful dinner parties and functions which remind me in many ways of my upbringing.

All families have their unique story and I'm proud of ours. To have travelled so far across the globe and Australia, I've been fortunate to have experiences that others have not. Writing this memoir has been a cathartic experience, allowing me to reflect on my life. I hope that by capturing it in these pages my grandchildren will be able to know some of the adventures of their Maa-Maa (Mama).

Conclusion

21 Davies St, Richmond Hill, Charters Towers

www.ingramcontent.com/pod-product-compliance
Lightning Source LLC
Chambersburg PA
CBHW041956080526
44588CB00021B/2758